THE
"I LOVE MY
AIR
FRYER"

EASY

RECIPES BOOK

THE "I LOVE MY AIR FRYER"

EASY

RECIPES BOOK

From *Pancake Muffins* to *Honey Balsamic Chicken Wings*,
175 Quick and Easy Recipes

Robin Fields
Author of The *"I Love My Air Fryer"*
5-Ingredient Recipe Book

Adams Media
New York   London   Toronto   Sydney   New Delhi

Adams Media
An Imprint of Simon & Schuster, LLC
100 Technology Center Drive
Stoughton, Massachusetts 02072

First Adams Media trade paperback edition April 2024

ADAMS MEDIA and colophon are registered trademarks of Simon & Schuster, LLC.

Simon & Schuster: Celebrating 100 Years of Publishing in 2024

For information about special discounts for bulk purchases, please contact Simon & Schuster Special Sales at 1-866-506-1949 or business@simonandschuster.com.

The Simon & Schuster Speakers Bureau can bring authors to your live event. For more information or to book an event, contact the Simon & Schuster Speakers Bureau at 1-866-248-3049 or visit our website at www.simonspeakers.com.

Interior design by Michelle Kelly
Photographs by James Stefiuk

Manufactured in the United States of America

1 2024

Library of Congress Cataloging-in-Publication Data
Names: Fields, Robin, author.
Title: The "I love my air fryer" easy recipes book / Robin Fields, Author of The "I Love My Air Fryer" 5-Ingredient Recipe Book
Description: Stoughton, Massachusetts: Adams Media, 2024. | Series: The "I love my" series | Includes index.
Identifiers: LCCN 2023044294 | ISBN 9781507221983 (pb) | ISBN 9781507221990 (ebook)
Subjects: LCSH: Hot air frying. | BISAC: COOKING / Methods / Special Appliances | COOKING / Methods / Frying | LCGFT: Cookbooks.
Classification: LCC TX689 .F543 2024 | DDC 641.7/7--dc23/eng/20231122
LC record available at https://lccn.loc.gov/2023044294

ISBN 978-1-5072-2198-3
ISBN 978-1-5072-2199-0 (ebook)

Always follow safety and commonsense cooking protocols while using kitchen utensils, operating ovens and stoves, and handling uncooked food. If children are assisting in the preparation of any recipe, they should always be supervised by an adult.

Contents

Introduction

Whether you're picking up an air fryer for the very first time or it's already your go-to tool in the kitchen, chances are you already have a good understanding of the influence this appliance has had in changing the way we cook. Air fryers continue to rise in popularity for a variety of reasons, from their ability to cook foods faster than traditional ovens to their unparalleled production of incredibly crispy dishes. Importantly, air fryers also make cooking easier than ever, opening the door for people of all skill levels to flex their culinary muscles and make good food fast.

Using an air fryer is a healthier way of enjoying your favorite fried foods than other cooking methods or takeout options. And it is an energy-efficient choice for those whose ovens tend to heat up their whole house in the warmer months. An air fryer can be a great alternative that takes much less time to preheat, less power to finish cooking, and less physical space than a traditional oven.

While using an air fryer saves you time, having a solid collection of recipes can make a world of a difference. Simple recipes, with easy-to-find ingredients and no more than five steps, are key to getting the most out of your air fryer. You don't need to spend more than 30 minutes in the kitchen to have a meal your whole family can enjoy, and The "*I Love My Air Fryer*" *Easy Recipes Book* will show you how to make this a reality.

The 175 delicious recipes that follow provide a wide range of dishes, including energizing breakfasts, snacks to tide you over between meals, sides to pair with any entrée, satisfying main courses, and impressive desserts your family will think you spent hours preparing. The entrées are organized into the categories of chicken, beef and pork, fish and seafood, and vegetarian dishes, so you can easily flip to whatever you are craving. You'll also find appetizing photos, along with several kitchen hacks and flavor substitutions to make cooking an even more convenient and customizable experience. Throughout this book, you'll learn everything you need to know about using an air fryer, as well as helpful ways get mouthwatering meals on the table in no time—even if you're completely new to cooking. It's time to get air frying!

Cooking with an Air Fryer

If you can press a button or turn a dial, then you can cook with an air fryer. If you're new to air fryer cooking, it might seem a bit intimidating, but truly, using your air fryer is just as easy as using a microwave. This chapter will introduce you to a range of air frying options, offer helpful hints to take with you on your air frying journey, and detail some of the must-have accessories that will greatly improve your cooking experience. This chapter will also serve as your go-to guide for the all-important task of keeping your air fryer clean. Taking good care of your appliance is essential to its longevity, and the better you maintain your air fryer, the longer you can rely on it to make easy and delicious meals at a moment's notice.

While this chapter covers the basics of air frying in general, the first step to understanding the ins and outs of this miraculous method of cooking is to read the manual that came with your air fryer. Air fryer popularity, as well as innovation, is at an all-time high, with no signs of slowing down. As a result, there are more varieties than ever, and each air fryer works a little bit differently. Understanding how to use your specific model is the key to success, and your manual will familiarize you with

troubleshooting tips as well as safety functions. Once you've read it, you're ready to get started on your cooking revolution.

Why Air Fry?

Air fryers have grown in popularity over the last several years because of the convenience they offer. From faster cook times to energy efficiency, air fryers offer so many advantages. Here are just a few of the reasons you'll want to expand your air frying experience:

- **Easy to use:** An air fryer can be a great tool for anyone who is new to cooking, doesn't have much time to prepare meals, or simply doesn't have space for an oven. Air fryers have very simple settings and straightforward controls that make for easy meal preparation.
- **Time saving:** Air fryers heat up a smaller cooking chamber than a traditional oven. This means they can circulate heat faster, leading to shorter cook times. An air fryer also takes less time to heat up than an oven, cutting your overall meal prep time even shorter.
- **An alternative to deep frying:** Deep frying gives foods a beautiful golden brown color and a satisfying crunch. While

these indulgences are tasty, they're not ideal for frequent consumption. Because of how air fryers circulate heat, you can get ultra-crispy foods without having to cook them in a pot of oil. Air fryer cooking requires less supervision during the cooking process than deep frying does, and the cleanup is much easier in comparison, making it ideal for busy weeknights.

- **Versatile:** Air fryers are not just for cooking vegetables and meat—they can also be used to make delicious, sweet treats. From breakfast to dessert, the air fryer can cook a wide range of dishes, keeping you satisfied for every meal.

Choosing an Air Fryer

When choosing an air fryer, it's important to pay attention to the sizes and temperature ranges of the models you're considering. Air fryer volume is usually measured in quarts. Sizes range from about 1.2 quarts, which can be useful for quickly cooking single-serve meals, to 10 or more quarts, which might be ideal for cooking dinner for a large family. Air fryers of at least 6 quarts are perfect for cooking dishes for a family of four. In fact, at this size, you can even roast an entire chicken. However, if you struggle to find open counter space and you're cooking for a much smaller crowd, a smaller air fryer can still give you all the power you need to whip up your favorite meals.

As for the temperature range, some air fryers will allow you to dehydrate foods at as low as 95°F, and others allow broiling all the way to 510°F. Depending on your own needs and preferences, you'll want to make sure your air fryer has the appropriate cooking capacity and temperature range.

As air fryer innovation continues, you can also find air fryer ovens, which come with multiple racks for cooking, much like standard ovens, and you can even buy outdoor air fryers that are capable of smoking food using wood pellets. The recipes in this book were developed and tested using a 6-quart-capacity air fryer with cooking temperatures between 320°F and 400°F.

The Functions of an Air Fryer

Most air fryers are outfitted with programmed buttons to help take the guesswork out of your dishes. They're helpful for everything from cooking up the crispiest chicken wings with the press of a button to roasting a flavorful salmon in the same manner.

These buttons are programmed with preset times and temperatures based on your specific air fryer model, and they can vary significantly. Because of the wide variety of air fryers available today, all the recipes in this book were created using manual times and temperatures and with an automatic preheat function. If your air fryer doesn't have an automatic preheat, allow 5 minutes of preheating at your desired temperature before cooking these recipes.

Essential Accessories

You might be surprised to know that just as an oven has helpful pans and accessories, an air fryer does too. Air fryers often come with a couple of accessories, such as a baking pan or rack, but as air fryers become more popular, the number of additional accessories you can find increases, making air frying easier than ever. These accessories broaden the repertoire of recipes you can make in your air fryer and open up options you never would've thought were possible. Here are some of the most common accessories for enhancing your air frying experience:

- **Metal rack.** Overcrowding the basket can affect that delicious crunch we all strive for. A common solution is to cook in batches, but, depending on the recipe, a rack may be a good alternative. It adds a layer to your cooking surface and maximizes the amount of food you can cook at once.
- **Skewer rack.** Kebabs are super delicious when made in the air fryer. To ensure that yours come out perfectly every time, you can purchase skewer racks to slightly elevate your kebabs for even roasting.
- **Ramekins.** Ramekins are useful in many types of recipes, from mini cakes to quiches. Small, 4" ramekins are ideal for a standard air fryer's cooking chamber. If they're oven safe, they're also safe to use in your air fryer.
- **Cake pans.** Cake pans are extremely useful in air fryer cooking. Beyond cakes, they also make the perfect all-purpose pan for dips, dishes with lots of sauce, and even cobblers. This book uses 6" round baking pans, but some air fryers

or air fryer ovens may be able to accommodate 8" pans.
- **Cupcake pans.** There are lots of options for cupcake pans in the air fryer. Many are silicone, and they come in a variety of sizes. Aluminum cupcake liners make a great alternative to cupcake pans. They're easy to find in the grocery store, and you can place them directly in the air fryer basket to quickly whip up a batch of fluffy muffins or moist cupcakes.
- **Basket liners.** Any type of parchment paper will work in the air fryer to ensure easy cleanup. You can cut your own to size, or choose from the many available precut options (some even with holes for steaming). Alternatively, you can use aluminum foil or a silicone liner made to fit an air fryer basket.
- **Cooking spray.** Although the air fryer cooks with little to no oil, there are some cases in which a little spray is necessary. When you make a breaded recipe, it's helpful to lightly spray oil on the breading to aid in browning and to keep it from sticking. As an alternative to store-bought cooking spray, try a reusable spray bottle filled with your own favorite oil.

Accessory Removal

Some pans can be more difficult to remove than others because of their size and the depth of the fryer basket. Here are some tools that will allow you to take dishes out of your appliance safely and easily:

- **Tongs.** These are useful for removing cooking pans that don't come with handles. They're also helpful for placing meat in the air fryer and lifting it out.
- **Oven mitts.** Sometimes simple is best. Your food will be very hot when you remove it, so it's great to have these around to protect your hands. Traditional oven mitts and silicone mitts are both great options.

Cleaning Your Air Fryer

Before cleaning your air fryer, it's important to make sure that the appliance is completely cool and unplugged. Some air fryers have more removable pieces than others, so always be sure to refer to the guide that came with your specific model for detailed instructions.

1. First, remove the air fryer rack from the bottom of the basket. This is typically a grate that can easily be taken out and washed with soap and warm water. If there is a lot of built-up grease, you can also let it soak. Avoid rough scouring pads, because they can affect nonstick coatings.

2. Next, the basket can be removed from the air fryer and wiped clean. It's important to never pour grease down the sink, because it can cause clogs. Pour any grease in the bottom of your air fryer into a safe container that you can throw away, such as an old coffee can. Once the grease has been wiped clean, you can wash the air fryer basket with soap and warm water. Pay extra attention to the underside of the basket and the outside walls where grease may have splattered.

3. Once your air fryer grate and basket have been washed, set them aside to air-dry. Wipe the outside of the air fryer clean with a damp cloth, and wipe the counter surrounding the area to avoid grease buildup.

4. Before replacing the clean, dry grate and basket, check inside the air fryer for pieces of food or grease. Use a damp cloth to remove any buildup, and check the heating element to ensure it's free of food.

5. Once everything has been cleaned and is completely dry, you can put all the elements back together so they're ready for your next cooking adventure.

Quick and Easy Cooking

Each recipe in this book is made up of simple, easy-to-find ingredients, has five or fewer steps, and takes 30 minutes or less from start to finish. These truly are the easiest recipes you can make in your air fryer. As you explore this collection of delicious dishes, a handful of tips will enhance your air frying experience, especially in relation to quickness and overall simplicity. Here are some ways to make your meals easier than ever:

- **Simplify your ingredients:** One of the most time-consuming parts of hands-on cooking is often chopping meat and vegetables. Save time by using pre-chopped ingredients from the grocery store. Alternatively, you can set aside time to chop vegetables in bulk and freeze them for later use.

- **Read the entire recipe:** Read the whole recipe before you begin cooking. Collect and prepare all the ingredients before beginning for a smooth cooking process.
- **Don't overcrowd the basket:** While it's tempting to fill up the basket, having too much food in the air fryer at once can hinder the airflow and affect the cook time. Always cook in batches when necessary, and upgrade your air fryer to a larger model if you find yourself constantly wishing for more space.
- **Use a food thermometer:** This is the best way to ensure all meat is cooked to a safe temperature to eat. While visual cues can be helpful, a meat thermometer is a more reliable test and is an essential tool for beginners.
- **Keep a close eye on the food:** Air fryers vary in fan strength and heat circulation, depending on their size and brand. Some may cook much faster than others, so it's best to keep a close eye on your food to ensure it's not overcooking. In a similar way, if the food looks like it's not quite done, always feel free to put it back in for a few minutes.
- **Clean regularly:** Regular cleaning is the best way to avoid buildup, which can affect the taste of your food and pose a fire hazard from the excessive grease. Using parchment paper or foil can also be a great time-saver. Just be sure to cut the pieces to fit your air fryer or purchase a precut air fryer liner. And remember to never place parchment or foil in the air fryer while preheating or

without food on top. Either material can fly into the heating element and cause a fire hazard.

- **Start small:** Find a few air fryer recipes you love, and keep making them. It will help you get comfortable with the air fryer, and if you're new to cooking, it can improve your confidence. Once you've got those recipes down, start trying new ones, and you'll be an air frying pro in no time.

With this chapter as your guide, you are ready to launch into an open sea of endless air fryer possibilities. The pages ahead are filled with delicious, easy recipes for every taste preference and appetite level. Use these recipes as a springboard, and always remember to let your creativity roam free in the kitchen. Season your dishes intuitively, and swap out ingredients where it makes sense for your own preferences.

2

Breakfast

Despite being the most important meal of the day, breakfast also tends to be the easiest meal to skip. The pressing tasks of getting ready for your day and heading out the door on schedule can leave you with little time to do much more than grab a bagel on your way out. But the good news is your air fryer can revolutionize breakfast time by helping you serve up morning meals that are consistently fast, flavorful, and family friendly. If you're ready to make over your mornings with time-saving treats, this chapter has everything you need. Whether you're looking for a savory start to your day like Cheesy Breakfast Popovers, or a sweet kick like Stuffed French Toast to help you get up and go, after diving into this chapter, your breakfast routine will never be the same.

Pancake Muffins

These muffins combine all the fluffy goodness of buttermilk pancakes with the quick and on-the-go convenience of breakfast muffins. Don't forget to drizzle them with maple syrup just before serving to add a familiar sweetness that takes them to the next level.

Hands-On Time: 5 minutes
Cook Time: 15 minutes

Yields 12

1½ cups all-purpose flour
¼ cup granulated sugar
¼ cup light brown sugar, packed
1 teaspoon baking powder
½ cup salted butter, melted
¼ cup buttermilk
1 large egg

CUSTOMIZE IT!

You can add your favorite mix-ins to flavor these muffins just like you would actual pancakes. Add ¼ cup semisweet chocolate chips to the batter for a chocolatey spin on the original recipe. Alternatively, ¼ cup chopped walnuts adds the perfect crunch!

1 Preheat air fryer to 300°F. In a large bowl, whisk together all ingredients until smooth and well combined.

2 Fill 12 silicone or aluminum muffin liners halfway, about 3 tablespoons of batter per cup.

3 Place cups in air fryer basket, working in batches as necessary. Cook 15 minutes, or until the edges are golden brown and a toothpick inserted into the center of a muffin comes out clean. Allow to cool 5 minutes before serving warm.

PER SERVING (SERVING SIZE: 1 MUFFIN)

CALORIES: 167 | FAT: 8g | SODIUM: 114mg | CARBOHYDRATES: 21g | FIBER: 0g | SUGAR: 9g | PROTEIN: 2g

Chewy Peanut Butter Granola Bars

For a quick, family-friendly breakfast that's packed with protein and just the right amount of chocolate to balance the flavor, these granola bars are the perfect choice. They're easy enough to make the morning of, or you can prepare them in advance for an equally tasty, grab-and-go start to your day.

Hands-On Time: 5 minutes
Cook Time: 12 minutes

Yields 6

1 large egg
¼ cup creamy peanut butter
¼ cup honey
¼ teaspoon ground cinnamon
¼ teaspoon vanilla extract
1 cup rolled oats

1 Preheat air fryer to 350°F. Line a 6" round baking pan with parchment paper and set aside.

2 In a large bowl, whisk egg, peanut butter, honey, cinnamon, and vanilla until smooth. Fold in oats. Scrape mixture into prepared pan and place in air fryer basket. Cook until edges are browned (12 minutes).

3 When done, carefully lift the parchment-lined bars out of the pan and place on a cooling rack. Allow to cool 45 minutes before slicing into 6 bars. Store leftovers in an airtight container in the refrigerator for up to 5 days.

PER SERVING (SERVING SIZE: 1 BAR)

CALORIES: 169 | FAT: 7g | SODIUM: 14mg | CARBOHYDRATES: 23g | FIBER: 2g | SUGAR: 13g | PROTEIN: 5g

Breakfast Burrito Bowls

Bring a Tex-Mex flair to your table with these satisfying and savory bowls. Complete with tortillas that crisp up beautifully in your air fryer basket, these loaded bowls are sure to become a part of your breakfast rotation. Customize the recipe by adding your favorite chopped vegetables, such as bell peppers and onions, and/or sliced avocado.

Hands-On Time: 5 minutes
Cook Time: 8 minutes per bowl

Serves 4

4 (8") flour tortillas
8 large eggs, whisked
½ teaspoon salt
¼ teaspoon ground black pepper
½ cup drained canned black beans
1 cup shredded Mexican-blend cheese

1 Preheat air fryer to 350°F. Nestle 1 tortilla into an ungreased 6" round baking pan. The edges of the tortilla will extend up the sides of the pan, creating a bowl shape.

2 Pour ¼ of the eggs into each bowl, sprinkle eggs with salt and pepper, and add black beans and cheese in an even layer on top.

3 Place pan in air fryer basket and cook 8 minutes, until eggs are firm and cheese is melted. Repeat with remaining tortillas and ingredients and serve warm.

PER SERVING

CALORIES: 414 | FAT: 19g | SODIUM: 905mg | CARBOHYDRATES: 31g | FIBER: 3g | SUGAR: 3g | PROTEIN: 25g

Stuffed French Toast

Stuffed French Toast is essentially a French toast sandwich, or in other words, a dream come true for many breakfast lovers. Chock-full of the flavors of cream cheese, cinnamon, and fresh strawberries, this is a breakfast you'll be happy to get out of bed for. Serve these up with a dusting of confectioners' sugar, a drizzle of maple syrup, or a spoonful of whipped cream.

Hands-On Time: 10 minutes
Cook Time: 12 minutes

Serves 4

- 2 ounces cream cheese, softened
- ½ cup granulated sugar, divided
- 1 teaspoon lemon juice
- 4 large eggs
- ½ cup whole milk
- 1 teaspoon ground cinnamon
- 8 slices thick-cut sandwich bread
- 4 medium strawberries, hulled and cut into ¼"-thick slices

1 Preheat air fryer to 370°F. In a medium bowl, mix cream cheese, ¼ cup sugar, and lemon juice. In a large bowl, whisk together eggs, milk, remaining ¼ cup sugar, and cinnamon.

2 On each slice of bread, spread a layer of cream cheese mixture. Arrange strawberry slices on 4 of the bread slices, on top of cream cheese mixture. Close sandwiches.

3 Dip each sandwich into milk and egg mixture, allowing it to soak in on each side. Place sandwiches in air fryer basket, and cook 12 minutes, turning halfway through cooking. When done, sandwiches will be golden brown. Let cool 5 minutes, then serve.

PER SERVING

CALORIES: 426 | FAT: 11g | SODIUM: 478mg | CARBOHYDRATES: 64g | FIBER: 2g | SUGAR: 32g | PROTEIN: 14g

Sweet Potato Breakfast Hash

This nutritious mix of savory ingredients comes together wonderfully in one pan for a hearty and satisfying meal. Add a fried egg on top for an extra boost of protein.

Hands-On Time: 10 minutes
Cook Time: 15 minutes

Serves 4

2 medium sweet potatoes, peeled and cut into ½" dice
4 ounces cremini mushrooms (also called baby bellas), cut into ¼"-thick slices
1 medium green bell pepper, seeded and diced
1 small yellow onion, peeled and diced
1 clove garlic, peeled and minced
1 tablespoon olive oil
1 teaspoon seasoned salt
¼ teaspoon ground black pepper

1 Preheat air fryer to 375°F. Place potatoes, mushrooms, bell pepper, onion, and garlic in a 6" round baking pan. Toss to combine.

2 Drizzle olive oil over vegetables and sprinkle with seasoned salt and ground black pepper. Place pan in air fryer and cook 15 minutes, until vegetables are tender and browned at edges. Serve.

PER SERVING

CALORIES: 101 | **FAT:** 3g | **SODIUM:** 403mg | **CARBOHYDRATES:** 16g | **FIBER:** 3g | **SUGAR:** 6g | **PROTEIN:** 2g

Fried Ham Steaks

Whether you're sliding it into a breakfast sandwich or enjoying it with a side of eggs, ham makes a great morning protein.

Hands-On Time: 5 minutes
Cook Time: 12 minutes

Serves 4

2 tablespoons salted butter, melted
2 tablespoons light brown sugar, packed
1 tablespoon pure maple syrup
1 pound ham steak

1 Preheat air fryer to 370°F. In a small bowl, mix butter, brown sugar, and maple syrup until well combined. Generously brush over ham steak on both sides.

2 Place ham steak in air fryer basket and cook 12 minutes, turning halfway through cooking time. When done, ham will be heated through and caramelized at edges from sugar. Slice and serve warm.

PER SERVING

CALORIES: 291 | **FAT:** 16g | **SODIUM:** 892mg | **CARBOHYDRATES:** 10g | **FIBER:** 0g | **SUGAR:** 10g | **PROTEIN:** 24g

Easy Breakfast Sandwiches

You'll find this recipe at the intersection of easy and portable. These sandwiches come together in just minutes and beat out any fast food alternative in both value and flavor. Feel free to swap out the ham for a sausage patty or enjoy these meatless.

Hands-On Time: 5 minutes
Cook Time: 8 minutes

Serves 4

4 white English muffins, split
8 (0.5-ounce) slices Black Forest ham
4 large eggs
¼ teaspoon salt
¼ teaspoon ground black pepper
4 (1-ounce) slices sharp Cheddar cheese

1 Preheat air fryer to 400°F. Once air fryer is preheated, place each English muffin, cut side up, in air fryer basket, working in batches as needed.

2 For each sandwich, place 2 slices of ham on one half of an English muffin. Crack an egg on top of the other muffin half. Sprinkle with salt and pepper. Cook 8 minutes, until eggs are fully cooked and English muffins are lightly browned.

3 Turn off air fryer, open basket, and place a slice of cheese on top of each egg. Close basket without turning on air fryer. Allow to rest in the residual heat until cheese is melted, about 2 minutes. Place a ham half and an egg half together to form each sandwich. Serve warm.

PER SERVING

CALORIES: 346 | **FAT:** 15g | **SODIUM:** 949mg | **CARBOHYDRATES:** 27g | **FIBER:** 2g | **SUGAR:** 3g | **PROTEIN:** 23g

Cheesy Breakfast Popovers

These light and airy popovers are the breakfast rolls your mornings have been missing. Made with no kneading and zero leavening agents, they still bake up tall and fluffy and, most importantly, very easily. Each cloudlike bite has a mild egg flavor that doesn't overpower the dish.

Hands-On Time: 5 minutes
Cook Time: 15 minutes

Yields 7

- ½ cup all-purpose flour
- ½ cup whole milk
- 2 large eggs, room temperature
- 2 tablespoons unsalted butter, melted and divided
- ½ teaspoon salt
- ¼ cup shredded sharp Cheddar cheese

1 Preheat air fryer to 370°F. Place a seven-well aluminum air fryer–style muffin pan in air fryer basket to preheat.

2 In a large bowl, whisk together flour, milk, eggs, 1 tablespoon butter, and salt until smooth and well combined. Stir in cheese.

3 Carefully pull out the fryer basket with hot muffin pan inside. Brush pan lightly with remaining 1 tablespoon butter. Fill each well of prepared muffin pan ⅔ full and push air fryer basket back in. Cook popovers 15 minutes, until they are browned and centers are set. Serve warm.

PER SERVING (SERVING SIZE: 1 POPOVER)

CALORIES: 108 | FAT: 6g | SODIUM: 220mg | CARBOHYDRATES: 8g | FIBER: 0g | SUGAR: 1g | PROTEIN: 4g

Blackberry-Baked Oatmeal

Baked oatmeal is a simple throw-it-together breakfast dish with a consistency reminiscent of bread pudding. In your air fryer, it cooks in just a fraction of the time it would take in your oven. Each bite is like a soft oatmeal cookie, full of warming spices that make this the perfect meal on cooler mornings. Sprinkle with sugar and extra blackberries for an even sweeter presentation.

Hands-On Time: 5 minutes
Cook Time: 15 minutes

Serves 4

1 cup rolled oats
½ cup pecans, chopped
2 large eggs
1 cup whole milk
¼ cup honey
3 tablespoons unsalted butter, melted
1 teaspoon vanilla extract
1 teaspoon ground cinnamon
½ teaspoon baking soda
1 cup fresh blackberries

1 Preheat air fryer to 320°F. Spray a 6" round baking pan with cooking spray and set aside.

2 In a large bowl, mix all ingredients except blackberries until well combined.

3 Fold in blackberries, then scrape mixture into prepared pan. Place pan in air fryer basket and cook 15 minutes, until oatmeal is browned on top and firm to the touch. Serve warm.

PER SERVING

CALORIES: 402 | FAT: 23g | SODIUM: 220mg | CARBOHYDRATES: 40g | FIBER: 6g | SUGAR: 24g | PROTEIN: 9g

TYPES OF OATS

The type of oats you use in recipes makes a big difference for the outcome. Instant and quick-cooking oats are rolled but cut into smaller pieces to promote faster cooking. If you use instant or quick-cooking oats in a recipe that calls for regular rolled oats, they will quickly overcook and turn gummy.

Cranberry Orange Muffins

Fresh cranberries can be hard to find outside of the holiday season, so be sure to save a couple cups and freeze them so you can make these muffins year-round.

Hands-On Time: 10 minutes
Cook Time: 15 minutes

Yields 12

1 cup all-purpose flour
½ cup granulated sugar
1 teaspoon baking powder
¼ cup salted butter, melted
1 large egg
½ cup whole milk
½ cup fresh cranberries, quartered
2 tablespoons orange zest

1 Preheat air fryer to 300°F. In a large mixing bowl, whisk together flour, sugar, and baking powder. Mix in butter, egg, and milk, and stir until well combined. Fold in cranberries and orange zest.

2 Fill 12 air fryer–safe aluminum muffin cups halfway. Place them in air fryer basket, working in batches as needed. Cook 15 minutes. Muffins will be browned at edges when done, and a toothpick inserted in a muffin's center will come out mostly clean.

PER SERVING (SERVING SIZE: 1 MUFFIN)

CALORIES: 119 | FAT: 4g | SODIUM: 81mg | CARBOHYDRATES: 18g | FIBER: 1g | SUGAR: 9g | PROTEIN: 2g

Chocolate Chip Muffins

Muffins are a great breakfast for all ages, and this simple recipe makes it easy to whip up a batch for breakfast or a sweet snack.

Hands-On Time: 15 minutes
Cook Time: 15 minutes

Yields 12

1 cup all-purpose flour
½ cup granulated sugar
1 teaspoon baking powder
1 large egg
1 cup whole milk
¼ cup salted butter, melted
⅓ cup semisweet chocolate chips

1 Preheat air fryer to 300°F. In a large bowl, whisk together flour, sugar, and baking powder. Add in egg, milk, and butter and mix until well combined. Fold in chocolate chips.

2 Divide batter evenly among 12 muffin cups, filling each no more than halfway. Place cups in air fryer basket, working in batches as needed. Cook 15 minutes, until muffins are browned on top and a toothpick inserted into center comes out clean. Serve warm.

PER SERVING (SERVING SIZE: 1 MUFFIN)

CALORIES: 113 | FAT: 3g | SODIUM: 56mg | CARBOHYDRATES: 21g | FIBER: 1g | SUGAR: 12g | PROTEIN: 2g

Dark Chocolate and Peanut Butter–Baked Oatmeal

Some of the best breakfasts are the ones that taste a little bit like dessert. This delectable baked oatmeal dish will get your day started on a sweet note while also including plenty of vitamins, thanks to the oats, and protein, courtesy of the peanut butter.

Hands-On Time: 5 minutes
Cook Time: 15 minutes

Serves 4

1½ cups rolled oats
1 large egg
1 cup whole milk
¼ cup light brown sugar, packed
¼ cup dark cocoa powder, sifted
3 tablespoons creamy peanut butter, melted
1 teaspoon vanilla extract
½ teaspoon baking soda
¼ cup semisweet chocolate chips

1 Preheat air fryer to 320°F. Spray a 6" round baking pan with cooking spray and set aside.

2 In a large bowl, mix all ingredients except chocolate chips until well combined. Fold in chocolate chips.

3 Scrape mixture into prepared baking pan and place in air fryer. Cook 15 minutes, until center is firm. Serve warm.

PER SERVING

CALORIES: 361 | FAT: 15g | SODIUM: 209mg | CARBOHYDRATES: 50g | FIBER: 6g | SUGAR: 25g | PROTEIN: 11g

Ham and Swiss Quiche

This savory breakfast pie offers a brilliant combination of delicious flavors and satisfying textures. From its flaky golden brown crust to its creamy filling, every bite is just as pleasing as the last. Serve with fresh fruit on the side for a colorful meal.

Hands-On Time: 5 minutes
Cook Time: 25 minutes

Serves 6

5 large eggs
½ cup heavy cream
1 cup shredded Swiss cheese
1 cup diced cooked ham
½ teaspoon salt
¼ teaspoon ground black pepper
1 (8-ounce) frozen savory pie crust in aluminum tin

CUSTOMIZE IT!

Ham and Swiss are used in this recipe, but feel free to swap in cooked crumbled sausage, bacon bits, or a mix of sautéed vegetables.

1 Preheat air fryer to 350°F.

2 In a large bowl, whisk eggs and cream together until smooth and well combined. Mix in cheese, ham, salt, and pepper until combined.

3 Parcook frozen pie crust in air fryer basket 5 minutes, until lightly browned. Pour egg mixture into crust and return to air fryer basket. Cook 20 minutes, until filling is firm and set in the center. Let cool 5 minutes before slicing, then serve warm.

PER SERVING

CALORIES: 426 | FAT: 27g | SODIUM: 772mg | CARBOHYDRATES: 23g | FIBER: 1g | SUGAR: 3g | PROTEIN: 18g

Sticky Bun Bites

Sticky buns are known for their delicious sauce, which coats the top of a sweetened dough roll. This shortcut recipe uses premade cinnamon rolls cut into bite-sized pieces for a quick and simple take on this cozy favorite. The brown sugar–based topping is deep and rich in flavor, pairing well with the cinnamon. This recipe includes pecans for an enjoyable crunch, but feel free to leave them out or switch them up for whatever nuts you have on hand.

Hands-On Time: 5 minutes
Cook Time: 8 minutes

Serves 8

- ⅓ cup light brown sugar, packed
- ¼ cup salted butter, cut into small cubes
- 1 teaspoon ground cinnamon
- ⅓ cup chopped pecans
- 1 (12.5-ounce) tube refrigerated cinnamon rolls

1 Preheat air fryer to 320°F. Place brown sugar, butter, and cinnamon in a small, heat-safe bowl. Microwave 45 seconds, until butter is fully melted, and stir until smooth.

2 Generously spray a 6" round baking pan with cooking spray. Scrape sugar mixture into pan and spread evenly across bottom of pan, then sprinkle pecans on top.

3 Cut each cinnamon roll into 4 even pieces, and scatter across top of sugar mixture and pecans.

4 Place pan in air fryer basket and cook 8 minutes, until cinnamon rolls are browned. Invert pan onto a serving plate so cinnamon rolls are on the bottom and covered with the sticky topping. Serve warm.

PER SERVING

CALORIES: 253 | FAT: 14g | SODIUM: 464mg | CARBOHYDRATES: 29g | FIBER: 2g | SUGAR: 12g | PROTEIN: 3g

Jumbo Cinnamon Roll Cake

Kick off a special day with Jumbo Cinnamon Roll Cake. It's a giant swirl that has layers of sweet, yeasted dough with cinnamon and sugar filling. To keep things easy, this recipe is made with a tube of cinnamon rolls so you can whip it up quickly and get back to enjoying your day. If you don't like much frosting, use the packet that comes with the cinnamon rolls and lightly drizzle on top. For a thicker coating, use the frosting in the recipe, and consider adding a few drops of food coloring for a festive presentation.

Hands-On Time: 10 minutes
Cook Time: 20 minutes

Serves 4

1 (12.5-ounce) tube refrigerated cinnamon rolls
¼ cup salted butter, softened
4 ounces cream cheese, softened
2 cups confectioners' sugar
1 tablespoon whole milk
1 tablespoon rainbow sprinkles

1 Preheat air fryer to 320°F. Cut a piece of parchment to fit air fryer basket.

2 Open tube of cinnamon rolls and place on a clean work surface. Unroll each cinnamon roll. Tightly reroll 1 cinnamon roll and place it on center of parchment. One after another, wrap remaining dough strips around center cinnamon roll, creating a single large spiral.

3 Place cake in air fryer basket and cook 20 minutes, until top is browned and dough is fully cooked through. Allow to cool 10 minutes before frosting.

4 To make frosting, beat butter and cream cheese in a large bowl until fluffy, 2–3 minutes. Add confectioners' sugar and milk until a smooth and silky frosting forms. Generously spread over cake and garnish with sprinkles to serve.

PER SERVING

CALORIES: 697 | **FAT:** 31g | **SODIUM:** 1,037mg | **CARBOHYDRATES:** 97g | **FIBER:** 2g | **SUGAR:** 64g | **PROTEIN:** 6g

Mixed Berry Pancake Bites

These bites are an excellent breakfast or snack for all ages.

Hands-On Time: 5 minutes
Cook Time: 8 minutes

Yields 12

1 cup self-rising flour
1 cup whole milk
1 large egg
½ cup mixed fresh berries

1 Preheat air fryer to 320°F. In a large bowl, whisk together flour, milk, and egg until a smooth batter forms.

2 Lightly spray silicone or aluminum baking cups with cooking spray and fill each halfway with pancake batter, about 3 tablespoons per cup. Gently press 2 berries into center of each cup until fully submerged.

3 Working in batches, place cups in air fryer basket and cook 8 minutes. When done, bites will be browned and an inserted toothpick will come out clean. Let cool 5 minutes and serve.

PER SERVING (SERVING SIZE: 3 BITES)

CALORIES: 173 | FAT: 3g | SODIUM: 416mg | CARBOHYDRATES: 28g | FIBER: 1g | SUGAR: 5g | PROTEIN: 7g

Chocolate-Baked Oats

This recipe uses bananas for sweetness. So, while decadent, it's a dish that you can feel good about eating.

Hands-On Time: 5 minutes
Cook Time: 10 minutes

Serves 4

2 cups rolled oats
1 cup whole milk
2 medium bananas
2 teaspoons baking powder
¼ cup cocoa powder
½ cup semisweet chocolate chips

1 Preheat air fryer to 350°F. Place all ingredients except chocolate chips in a blender and blend for 30 seconds, until mostly smooth.

2 Spray four 4" ramekins with nonstick cooking spray, and pour oat mixture evenly into each ramekin. Top each ramekin with chocolate chips and place in air fryer basket, working in batches.

3 Cook 10 minutes, until edges are set and a toothpick inserted into the center comes out clean. Allow baked oats to cool 5 minutes, then serve.

PER SERVING

CALORIES: 361 | FAT: 12g | SODIUM: 273mg | CARBOHYDRATES: 62g | FIBER: 9g | SUGAR: 24g | PROTEIN: 10g

Espresso Cream Cheese Danish

If you like coffee-flavored cheesecake, you'll love this Danish. This nontraditional treat pairs the rich flavor of espresso with a creamy filling for a unique dessert. Instant espresso powder is used for bold flavor, but instant coffee will work as well.

Hands-On Time: 10 minutes
Cook Time: 15 minutes

Serves 8

4 ounces cream cheese, softened

¼ cup light brown sugar, packed

1 teaspoon instant espresso powder

½ teaspoon vanilla extract

1 (13.2-ounce) package puff pastry, thawed

1 large egg, whisked

1 Preheat air fryer to 320°F. In a medium bowl, mix cream cheese, brown sugar, espresso powder, and vanilla until well combined.

2 On a clean work surface, unroll puff pastry and cut into 8 rectangles. Poke with a fork to prevent puffing.

3 Place 2 tablespoons filling in center of each puff pastry rectangle. Fold and press each corner in toward the center ½", leaving filling uncovered. Brush edges of exposed puff pastry with egg wash.

4 Place Danishes in air fryer basket, working in batches as needed. Cook 15 minutes. When done, puff pastry will be golden brown and filling will be set. Let cool 5 minutes and serve.

PER SERVING

CALORIES: 255 | FAT: 16g | SODIUM: 222mg | CARBOHYDRATES: 22g | FIBER: 0g | SUGAR: 8g | PROTEIN: 4g

Breakfast Pigs in a Blanket

This recipe is a morning lifesaver and can even be prepared ahead of time. Picky eaters will love these breakfast sausages wrapped in buttery dough. They come together quickly and make a great on-the-go meal for busy days. For a sweet spin, use premade cinnamon rolls instead of crescent roll dough and use maple-flavored breakfast sausage. Enjoy alongside syrup for dipping.

Hands-On Time: 5 minutes
Cook Time: 8 minutes

Serves 8

1 (8-ounce) tube refrigerated crescent roll dough
8 (0.8-ounce) raw breakfast sausage links

1. Preheat air fryer to 350°F.

2. On a clean work surface, unroll dough and separate into triangles. Place 1 sausage along widest side of each triangle and roll up, wrapping sausages in dough.

3. Place pigs in a blanket in air fryer basket and cook 8 minutes, turning halfway through cooking time. When done, sausages will have an internal temperature of at least 160°F and crescent rolls will be golden brown on outside. Serve warm.

PER SERVING

CALORIES: 180 | FAT: 12g | SODIUM: 392mg | CARBOHYDRATES: 12g | FIBER: 0g | SUGAR: 3g | PROTEIN: 5g

Banana Peanut Butter Breakfast Cookies

Breakfast cookies are an excellent way to fuel your day. They can be prepared and stored in the refrigerator all week and make an excellent grab-and-go meal. Feel free to add nuts to these or swap the peanut butter for almond butter or sunflower butter. Be sure to use very ripe bananas for the sweetest taste and best texture.

Hands-On Time: 5 minutes
Cook Time: 12 minutes

Yields 6

2 medium bananas
2 cups rolled oats
½ cup smooth peanut butter
½ teaspoon ground cinnamon

1 Preheat air fryer to 320°F. Cut a piece of parchment paper to fit air fryer and set aside.

2 In a large bowl, mash bananas until no large chunks remain. Add remaining ingredients and stir until well combined.

3 Separate dough into 6 even portions, and roll each into a ball. Press each ball gently to form a flat disc about ½" thick. Place discs on parchment paper, at least 1" apart.

4 Cook 12 minutes, until cookies' centers appear firm and edges are set. Let cool 5 minutes before serving.

PER SERVING (SERVING SIZE: 1 COOKIE)

CALORIES: 264 | FAT: 12g | SODIUM: 91mg | CARBOHYDRATES: 32g | FIBER: 5g | SUGAR: 8g | PROTEIN: 9g

Blueberry Bread Pudding

This breakfast bread pudding is bursting with fruit flavor. A morning spin on bread pudding, it uses flaky, buttery croissants as a base. This is a great way to use croissants that are a day or two old. Finish with a dusting of confectioners' sugar, if you desire, for a photo-worthy finish.

Hands-On Time: 5 minutes
Cook Time: 25 minutes

Serves 4

- 3 large eggs, room temperature
- 1 cup heavy cream
- ½ cup light brown sugar, packed
- 1 teaspoon vanilla extract
- 1 teaspoon ground cinnamon
- 2 tablespoons salted butter, melted
- 3 medium croissants, cut into 1" cubes
- 1 cup fresh blueberries

1 Preheat air fryer to 350°F. Spray a 6" round baking pan with nonstick cooking spray and set aside.

2 In a medium bowl, whisk together eggs, cream, brown sugar, vanilla, cinnamon, and melted butter until well combined and smooth.

3 Gently fold croissant cubes and blueberries into egg mixture, then scrape into prepared baking pan. Cook 25 minutes, until edges are set and top is golden brown. Let cool 10 minutes before slicing. Serve warm.

PER SERVING

CALORIES: 580 | FAT: 34g | SODIUM: 299mg | CARBOHYDRATES: 55g | FIBER: 2g | SUGAR: 37g | PROTEIN: 10g

CUSTOMIZE IT!

Make this dish your own by swapping out the blueberries for blackberries, strawberries, or raspberries. Chocolate lovers may enjoy a sprinkling of chocolate chips as an alternative.

Nutella French Toast Roll-Ups

If you don't already believe chocolate hazelnut spread makes everything better, let this indulgent breakfast treat change your mind. An enhancement of your usual French toast, this is one recipe that will be gobbled up even faster than you can cook more.

Hands-On Time: 10 minutes
Cook Time: 5 minutes

Yields 8

8 slices white sandwich bread, crusts removed
½ cup Nutella chocolate hazelnut spread
3 large eggs
¼ cup whole milk
1 teaspoon vanilla extract
3 tablespoons unsalted butter, melted
¼ cup granulated sugar
1 tablespoon ground cinnamon

1 Preheat air fryer to 375°F.

2 With a rolling pin or your hands, flatten each slice of bread to a ¼" thickness. Spread 1 tablespoon Nutella along an edge of a bread slice, and roll tightly to close. Repeat with remaining slices.

3 In a medium-sized bowl, whisk together eggs, milk, and vanilla until well combined. Carefully dip each roll-up into egg mixture until bread is well saturated.

4 Place each roll-up in air fryer basket. Air fry 5 minutes, turning halfway through cooking time. When done, roll-ups will be golden brown. Use tongs to transfer roll-ups to a plate, and brush each with butter.

5 In a small bowl, whisk together sugar and cinnamon. Place each roll-up in mixture and gently press to coat with cinnamon and sugar. Serve warm.

PER SERVING (SERVING SIZE: 2 ROLL-UPS)

CALORIES: 549 | FAT: 24g | SODIUM: 359mg | CARBOHYDRATES: 66g | FIBER: 4g | SUGAR: 38g | PROTEIN: 13g

3

Appetizers and Snacks

When you need a small bite in between meals or something tasty to ease your appetite before the main course, appetizers and snacks always come in handy. These dishes are excellent to serve for everything from big game-day events to intimate get-togethers. Gathering over good food always makes spending time together even more enjoyable. And your air fryer makes it quick and easy to put together these mini meals without any hassle. From Creamy Layered Pizza Dip to Bacon-Wrapped Dates, this chapter is abuzz with palatable plates that will make snack time fun!

Bacon-Wrapped Dates

Medjool dates are a naturally sweet, soft, and chewy fruit with a slightly caramelized taste. This flavor and texture combination pairs perfectly with salty, savory, crispy bacon, creating a delicious and elegant appetizer with full-bodied flavor.

Hands-On Time: 10 minutes
Cook Time: 8 minutes

Serves 6

12 medium Medjool dates, pitted
3 ounces soft goat cheese
6 slices bacon, cut in half crosswise

1   Preheat air fryer to 350°F.

2   Slice each date open on one side. Use 1½ teaspoons goat cheese to fill each date.

3   Wrap each date in a half-slice of bacon and secure with a toothpick. Place wrapped dates in air fryer basket. Air fry 8 minutes, until bacon is browned and fully cooked. Serve warm.

PER SERVING

CALORIES: 227 | FAT: 7g | SODIUM: 221mg | CARBOHYDRATES: 36g | FIBER: 3g | SUGAR: 32g | PROTEIN: 7g

Baked Brie with Honey and Walnuts

Brie doesn't need a lot of help to become a sophisticated appetizer, but gentle cooking and the addition of complementary flavors will turn a simple block of cheese into the crowd-pleasing star of your next snack table.

Hands-On Time: 5 minutes
Cook Time: 7 minutes

Serves 8

1 (8-ounce) wheel Brie cheese
¼ teaspoon salt
½ cup shelled walnuts, roughly chopped
⅓ cup honey

1   Preheat air fryer to 350°F. Spray a 6" round baking pan with cooking spray and set aside.

2   Use a knife to cut top of Brie rind off about ¼" deep to expose creamy interior, and discard cut rind. Place Brie in prepared pan. Sprinkle with salt, then with walnuts.

3   Place pan in air fryer basket. Cook 7 minutes, until walnuts are toasted and Brie is creamy. Drizzle honey on top and over the sides, then serve warm.

PER SERVING

CALORIES: 179 | FAT: 12g | SODIUM: 240mg | CARBOHYDRATES: 13g | FIBER: 1g | SUGAR: 12g | PROTEIN: 7g

Crispy Fried Burrata

Though mild in flavor, burrata is really at its best when coated in panko, or crisp, dry crumbs made from crustless white bread, and lightly fried. Traditional frying methods can easily lead to overcooking, but your air fryer makes it simple.

Hands-On Time: 10 minutes
Cook Time: 5 minutes

Serves 8

½ cup all-purpose flour
¼ teaspoon salt
¼ teaspoon ground black pepper
1 large egg
½ cup Italian-style panko
8 ounces burrata

1 Preheat air fryer to 400°F.

2 Use three medium bowls for dredging. In first bowl, whisk together flour, salt, and pepper. In second bowl, whisk egg, and in final bowl, place panko.

3 Gently roll burrata in flour to evenly coat. Next, coat in egg and allow excess to drip off. Finally, gently roll in panko, coating as evenly as possible. Spray lightly with cooking spray.

4 Place breaded burrata in the air fryer basket and cook 5 minutes, turning when 2 minutes remain. Burrata will be golden brown when done. Use a spatula to carefully lift it out of the basket and place it on a cutting board. Allow at least 5 minutes to cool, then use a large knife to slice. Serve immediately while very warm.

PER SERVING

CALORIES: 126 | FAT: 8g | SODIUM: 133mg | CARBOHYDRATES: 7g | FIBER: 1g | SUGAR: 0g | PROTEIN: 6g

Spinach and Feta Phyllo Cups

A creamy savory spinach filling meets a flaky phyllo shell in this simple and portable appetizer. Cooked until browned and bubbling, each mouthwatering cup tastes as irresistible as it looks.

Hands-On Time: 10 minutes
Cook Time: 7 minutes

Serves 5

2 ounces cream cheese, softened
¼ cup crumbled feta cheese
1 cup loosely packed fresh spinach, finely chopped
1 clove garlic, peeled and finely minced
¼ teaspoon crushed red pepper flakes
¼ teaspoon salt
1 (1.9-ounce) package frozen mini phyllo shells

1 Preheat air fryer to 375°F. In a large bowl, mix cream cheese, feta, spinach, garlic, red pepper flakes, and salt until well combined.

2 Place 1 tablespoon of mixture in center of each phyllo cup. Place cups in air fryer basket. Cook 7 minutes, until cups are browned and spinach mixture is bubbling. Serve warm.

PER SERVING

CALORIES: 106 | **FAT:** 6g | **SODIUM:** 269mg | **CARBOHYDRATES:** 7g | **FIBER:** 0g | **SUGAR:** 1g | **PROTEIN:** 3g

Fried Cheese Curds

You might have enjoyed fried cheese curds at a local fair, but did you know that they're incredibly simple to make at home in your air fryer? Skip the mess and difficulty of dealing with hot oil and try these crisp, golden brown flavor-filled treats whenever your cheese cravings strike.

Hands-On Time: 10 minutes
Cook Time: 8 minutes

Serves 8

1 cup all-purpose flour
¼ teaspoon garlic salt
¼ teaspoon salt
1 large egg, whisked
1 cup plain panko
1 pound Cheddar cheese curds

1 Preheat air fryer to 350°F. In one medium bowl, whisk flour with garlic salt and salt. In another medium bowl, place whisked egg. Place panko in a third medium bowl.

2 Working in batches, dip cheese curds in flour to evenly coat. Next, dip in egg and allow excess to drip off. Finally, dip in panko, coating curds as evenly as possible. Lightly spray coated cheese curds with cooking spray.

3 Place cheese curds in air fryer basket and cook 8 minutes, until golden brown and crispy. Serve warm.

PER SERVING

CALORIES: 309 | FAT: 17g | SODIUM: 528mg | CARBOHYDRATES: 18g | FIBER: 0g | SUGAR: 1g | PROTEIN: 15g

Cheesy Bean Dip

If you're looking for a more creative companion to your tortilla chips than the usual queso, give this recipe a try. It's the perfect game-day treat, complete with a satisfying blend of flavors and a customizable level of spice, depending on the taco seasoning and salsa you choose to include.

Hands-On Time: 5 minutes
Cook Time: 12 minutes

Serves 6

- 1 (16-ounce) can refried beans
- ¾ cup sour cream
- 4 ounces cream cheese, softened
- 2 tablespoons premade taco seasoning
- ¾ cup shredded Mexican-blend cheese, divided
- ¼ cup mild salsa

1 Preheat air fryer to 350°F. Spray a 6" round baking pan with cooking spray and set aside.

2 Mix refried beans, sour cream, cream cheese, and taco seasoning in a medium bowl until smooth and well combined. Mix ½ cup shredded cheese and salsa in a separate medium bowl, then stir into bean mixture until well combined.

3 Scrape bean mixture into prepared baking pan and top with remaining ¼ cup shredded cheese. Place pan in air fryer and bake 12 minutes, until cheese is melted and edges are bubbling. Serve.

PER SERVING

CALORIES: 249 | FAT: 15g | SODIUM: 691mg | CARBOHYDRATES: 14g | FIBER: 4g | SUGAR: 3g | PROTEIN: 9g

Creamy Layered Pizza Dip

This hot and cheesy dip brings all the best parts of a pizza to your baking pan. Begging to be devoured with a toasted slice of your favorite crusty bread, this is definitely one of those appetizers that can easily be enjoyed as a whole meal.

Hands-On Time: 5 minutes
Cook Time: 15 minutes

Serves 8

- 4 ounces cream cheese, softened
- ¼ cup ricotta cheese
- ¼ cup plus 2 tablespoons grated Parmesan cheese, divided
- 2 teaspoons Italian seasoning
- ¼ teaspoon salt
- 1½ cups shredded mozzarella cheese, divided
- 1 cup pizza sauce
- 20 slices pepperoni, quartered and divided

DIPPERS

Pieces of French bread, pita chips, and even cut-up premade pizza crust are great options for dipping. Small naan bites and bread bites are also excellent options and hold up well to this dish's sauce and toppings.

1 Preheat air fryer to 320°F. Spray a 6" round baking pan with cooking spray.

2 In a large bowl, beat cream cheese, ricotta, ¼ cup Parmesan, Italian seasoning, and salt until well combined. Scrape cheese mixture into prepared pan.

3 Spread cheese mixture in an even layer, and sprinkle evenly with ½ cup mozzarella. Next, pour pizza sauce on top in an even layer and top with pepperoni, reserving a few pieces of pepperoni.

4 Place remaining 1 cup mozzarella and remaining 2 tablespoons Parmesan on top of sauce and pepperoni layers, then top with remaining pepperoni. Place pan in air fryer basket and cook 15 minutes, until cheese is melted and sauce is bubbling at the sides. Serve warm.

PER SERVING

CALORIES: 170 | FAT: 11g | SODIUM: 517mg | CARBOHYDRATES: 5g | FIBER: 1g | SUGAR: 2g | PROTEIN: 9g

Avocado Fries

These fries are creamy on the inside with a crisp and golden exterior. While avocados tend to have a mild taste when enjoyed raw, cooking them brings out their nutty flavor, which pairs perfectly with these fries' Parmesan coating.

Hands-On Time: 10 minutes
Cook Time: 8 minutes

Serves 4

½ cup all-purpose flour
1 large egg, whisked
½ cup plain panko
½ cup grated Parmesan cheese
4 medium avocados, pitted, peeled, and sliced into ¼"-thick spears

1 Preheat air fryer to 375°F. Place flour in one medium bowl, egg in another medium bowl, and panko mixed with Parmesan in a third medium bowl.

2 Dip each avocado slice in flour, then in egg. Allow excess egg to drip off, then gently press into panko and cheese mixture so that each slice is well coated.

3 Spray coated slices lightly with cooking spray and place in air fryer basket. Cook 8 minutes, until golden. Serve warm.

PER SERVING

CALORIES: 404 | FAT: 23g | SODIUM: 281mg | CARBOHYDRATES: 36g | FIBER: 10g | SUGAR: 1g | PROTEIN: 11g

CHOOSING AN AVOCADO

Avocados soften when cooked, meaning the best avocados to use for this recipe are firm. If you begin with overly ripe avocados, it's likely they will become too soft. Look for those just under ripe, with firm skin that allows you to press it in only a little.

Ham and Cheese–Baked Pinwheels

These pinwheels are both family friendly and crowd-pleasing. Featuring the classic flavor combination of ham and cheese, they come together very simply. Feel free to switch up the flavors. Try turkey and Cheddar, roast beef and Swiss, or a new combination all your own.

Hands-On Time: 5 minutes
Cook Time: 8 minutes

Serves 4

1 (13.8-ounce) tube refrigerated pizza dough
2 tablespoons all-purpose flour
2 tablespoons yellow mustard
¼ pound Black Forest ham, thinly sliced
¼ pound mild Cheddar cheese, thinly sliced
1 large egg, whisked
1 teaspoon poppy seeds

1 Preheat air fryer to 350°F. Unroll pizza dough on a clean work surface lightly dusted with flour. Roll dough out to ¼" thickness.

2 Brush dough lightly with mustard, then place a layer of ham on top, followed by a layer of Cheddar, leaving a 1" border around the edges.

3 Starting at a short end, roll dough into a log. Press to seal, and place log seam-side down on work surface. Using a sharp knife, cut into 8 sections, each 1" thick.

4 Brush top and sides of each pinwheel with a light layer of egg wash, and sprinkle lightly with poppy seeds. Place pinwheels in air fryer basket and cook 8 minutes, turning when 2 minutes of cooking time remain. When done, dough will be browned and cooked through. Serve warm.

PER SERVING

CALORIES: 425 | FAT: 14g | SODIUM: 1,166mg | CARBOHYDRATES: 51g | FIBER: 2g | SUGAR: 7g | PROTEIN: 21g

Chili Lime Crunchy Chickpeas

Air-fried chickpeas are a crunchy and salty snack that makes a nutritious alternative to popcorn or potato chips. They can be flavored in a variety of ways but are especially delicious with a bit of spice. To ramp up this recipe's spiciness, try tossing in ¼ teaspoon of cayenne pepper.

Hands-On Time: 5 minutes
Cook Time: 15 minutes

Serves 4

2 (15-ounce) cans chickpeas, drained, rinsed, and patted dry
1 tablespoon olive oil
1 teaspoon salt
2 teaspoons ground cumin
1 teaspoon chili powder
Zest of 1 small lime

1 Preheat air fryer to 400°F.

2 In a medium bowl, toss chickpeas in olive oil. Sprinkle with salt, cumin, and chili powder. Sprinkle lime zest over chickpeas and toss to combine.

3 Place chickpeas in air fryer basket and cook 15 minutes, shaking basket twice during cooking. When done, chickpeas will be crunchy and browned. Serve warm.

PER SERVING

CALORIES: 220 | FAT: 6g | SODIUM: 884mg | CARBOHYDRATES: 31g | FIBER: 9g | SUGAR: 5g | PROTEIN: 10g

Bagel Chips

Crispy and delicious bagel chips are the perfect snack for all ages. This recipe works well for both fresh bagels and those that are a day or two old and have lost some moisture. They toast up into amazing, crunchy pieces that make the perfect dippers for whipped cream cheese or your favorite warm dips. Feel free to add herbs and spices on top of bagel slices before frying for a more robust flavor.

Hands-On Time: 5 minutes
Cook Time: 5 minutes

Serves 4

4 bakery-sized plain bagels, sliced vertically into ¼"-thick rounds
2 tablespoons olive oil

SERVING SUGGESTIONS

Switch up the flavor profile of this recipe by using different flavors of bagels. You can also try out different flavors of cream cheese for dipping or spreading or add seasoning to the cream cheese to shake things up. Everything bagel seasoning, mixed herb seasoning, or even a drizzle of honey can liven things up, too, and make a satisfying pairing for the chips.

1 Preheat air fryer to 370°F.

2 Lightly brush bagel pieces with olive oil and place in a single layer in air fryer basket. Cook 5 minutes, turning pieces when 2 minutes of cook time remain. When done, bagel chips will be golden and toasted. Serve warm.

PER SERVING

CALORIES: 419 | FAT: 8g | SODIUM: 699mg | CARBOHYDRATES: 70g | FIBER: 3g | SUGAR: 0g | PROTEIN: 14g

Cinnamon Sugar Tortilla Chips

The air fryer is great for making homemade tortilla chips, and why stop at plain ones? Adding cinnamon and sugar makes for delightfully sweet chips that you can enjoy with your sweet dips, fruit salsas, and even ice cream!

Hands-On Time: 5 minutes
Cook Time: 5 minutes

Serves 4

4 (6") flour tortillas
4 tablespoons unsalted butter, melted
⅓ cup granulated sugar
1 tablespoon ground cinnamon

FRUIT SALAD

These sweet chips are perfect for eating with fruit salad. Dice up your favorite fruits and drizzle with a couple of tablespoons of honey for a quick and easy fresh-tasting snack. Apples, berries, kiwi, pineapple, grapes, oranges, and melon cut into small pieces all work well in fruit salad.

1 Preheat air fryer to 320°F. Cut each tortilla into 6 even pieces. Lightly brush each piece with butter.

2 Place sugar and cinnamon in a large sealable bag. Working in batches, place tortilla pieces in bag and shake to coat in cinnamon and sugar mixture.

3 Place tortillas in air fryer in a single layer and cook 5 minutes, until crispy and browned, working in batches as needed. Store leftovers in an airtight container for up to 2 days.

PER SERVING

CALORIES: 207 | **FAT:** 7g | **SODIUM:** 213mg | **CARBOHYDRATES:** 34g | **FIBER:** 2g | **SUGAR:** 18g | **PROTEIN:** 3g

Roasted Pumpkin Seeds

Typically roasted in the oven for around 45 minutes, pumpkin seeds in the air fryer take a fraction of the time. Roasting brings out the seeds' natural nutty flavor and gives them an amazing crunch that serves as a satisfying snack, textured salad addition, or chopped and sprinkled topping for vegetables.

Hands-On Time: 5 minutes
Cook Time: 15 minutes

Serves 8

2 cups raw pumpkin seeds
2 teaspoons olive oil
1 teaspoon seasoned salt

1 Preheat air fryer to 350°F. Place pumpkin seeds in a 6" round baking pan and drizzle with olive oil.

2 Sprinkle seasoned salt on top of seeds and gently stir to coat. Cook 15 minutes, stirring twice during cooking. When done, the shells will be crunchy and easy to break or bite into. Serve warm. Store leftovers in an airtight container in the refrigerator for up to 2 weeks.

PER SERVING

CALORIES: 81 | FAT: 4g | SODIUM: 192mg | CARBOHYDRATES: 9g | FIBER: 3g | SUGAR: 0g | PROTEIN: 3g

Small-Batch Croutons

These croutons are the perfect way to use up those last pieces of bread that have lost their moisture but not their flavor. The pieces of bread toast up to a golden brown hue that's hard to resist. They can be used to add texture to salad or simply enjoyed as a poppable snack.

Hands-On Time: 5 minutes
Cook Time: 5 minutes

Serves 8

2 cups 1" French bread cubes made from day-old bread
1 tablespoon olive oil
¼ teaspoon salt

1 Preheat air fryer to 375°F.

2 Place bread in a medium bowl and drizzle with olive oil. Sprinkle salt on top and toss to coat.

3 Place bread in air fryer basket and cook 5 minutes, shaking basket halfway through cooking time. When done, croutons will be golden brown and crispy. Let cool 5 minutes and serve.

PER SERVING

CALORIES: 61 | FAT: 2g | SODIUM: 174mg | CARBOHYDRATES: 9g | FIBER: 0g | SUGAR: 1g | PROTEIN: 2g

Sweet and Spicy Party Nuts

Nuts make a great appetizer and charcuterie board staple, and this recipe elevates them with a sweet and spicy twist. Three types of nuts come together for a variety of textures and flavors. Feel free to substitute 2 cups of packaged mixed nuts to make this recipe even easier.

Hands-On Time: 5 minutes
Cook Time: 8 minutes

Serves 8

1 cup unsalted roasted peanuts
½ cup unsalted roasted cashews
½ cup raw pecans
½ teaspoon salt
¼ teaspoon cayenne pepper
2 tablespoons salted butter
2 tablespoons light brown sugar, packed

1 Preheat air fryer to 350°F. Cut a piece of parchment to fit air fryer basket and set aside.

2 In a large bowl, mix peanuts, cashews, and pecans. Sprinkle with salt and cayenne and toss until evenly coated.

3 Place butter and brown sugar in a small, heat-safe bowl. Microwave 45 seconds, then stir until sugar is fully dissolved. Pour over nuts and toss to combine.

4 Place parchment in air fryer basket. Scrape mixture onto parchment and spread nuts in a single layer. Cook 8 minutes, stirring twice during cooking. When done, nuts will be fragrant and soft.

5 Spread nuts on a clean piece of parchment to cool at least 15 minutes. Store leftovers in an airtight container on the counter for up to a week.

PER SERVING

CALORIES: 237 | FAT: 19g | SODIUM: 171mg | CARBOHYDRATES: 11g | FIBER: 2g | SUGAR: 5g | PROTEIN: 6g

Chex Mix

This party staple comes together in no time. Filled with a mix of salty and savory components, this snack has something everyone will love. It's also an excellent way to use up leftover partially finished snacks and revive them with a subtle buttery flavor that will keep everyone coming back for more.

Hands-On Time: 5 minutes
Cook Time: 12 minutes

Serves 8

1½ cups Corn Chex
1 cup Wheat Chex
¾ cup pretzel twists
¾ cup Cheez-It Original cheese crackers
5 tablespoons salted butter, melted
1 (1-ounce) packet ranch seasoning

1 Preheat air fryer to 300°F.

2 In a large bowl, mix Chex cereals, pretzels, and crackers. Pour butter over mix and toss to coat as evenly as possible. Sprinkle ranch powder onto mixture and toss until all pieces are coated.

3 Place in air fryer basket and cook 12 minutes, shaking basket three times during cooking. When done, mix will be slightly toasted and browned. Spread mixture out on a baking sheet to cool 10 minutes before serving. Store leftovers in an airtight container on the counter for up to 3 days.

PER SERVING

CALORIES: 165 | FAT: 9g | SODIUM: 519mg | CARBOHYDRATES: 20g | FIBER: 2g | SUGAR: 1g | PROTEIN: 2g

Barbecue Chicken Flatbread Pizza

Flatbread pizza is an excellent meal shortcut for those who don't want to use traditional pizza dough. Naan, a type of flatbread with roots in India, has a charred flavor, making it the ideal choice for a barbecue pizza. The multilayered smoky flavors contrast gorgeously with the bright freshness of red onion and cilantro.

Hands-On Time: 5 minutes
Cook Time: 10 minutes

Serves 4

- 4 precooked naan
- 1 cup plus 2 tablespoons barbecue sauce, divided
- 2 cups shredded mozzarella cheese
- 2 cups diced cooked chicken breast
- ¼ medium red onion, peeled and cut into ¼" slices
- 2 tablespoons chopped fresh cilantro

1 Preheat air fryer to 375°F.

2 Place flatbreads on a clean work surface. Spoon ¼ cup barbecue sauce onto each flatbread. On each pizza, evenly sprinkle ½ cup cheese on top of barbecue sauce and top with ½ cup chicken and a few red onion slices.

3 Working in batches as needed, place each pizza in air fryer basket and cook 10 minutes, until cheese is melted and bubbling. Drizzle with remaining 2 tablespoons barbecue sauce, garnish with cilantro, and serve.

PER SERVING

CALORIES: 766 | FAT: 19g | SODIUM: 2,156mg | CARBOHYDRATES: 99g | FIBER: 3g | SUGAR: 34g | PROTEIN: 45g

Tangy Sriracha Turkey Meatballs

Turkey meatballs are a great party food and a light alternative to beef. This recipe features sweet, glazed meatballs with a spicy kick that are sure to be an instant crowd-pleaser. The glaze adds moisture to the meatballs, so you won't even need a dipping sauce for this simple dish.

Hands-On Time: 10 minutes
Cook Time: 12 minutes

Serves 8

1½ pounds 85% lean ground turkey
¼ cup plain panko
1 teaspoon salt
½ teaspoon garlic powder
¼ teaspoon ground ginger
½ cup sriracha
¼ cup honey
3 tablespoons soy sauce
2 tablespoons rice vinegar
1 tablespoon sesame seeds
1 medium green onion, thinly sliced

1 Preheat air fryer to 350°F. In a large bowl, mix turkey, panko, salt, garlic powder, and ginger until well combined.

2 Form meatballs using 2-tablespoon scoops of meat. Spray air fryer basket with nonstick cooking spray and place meatballs in air fryer basket. Cook 10 minutes.

3 While meatballs are cooking, whisk together sriracha, honey, soy sauce, and vinegar in a small bowl until well combined, then set aside.

4 When meatballs have cooked 10 minutes, remove from air fryer and transfer to a 6" round baking pan. Pour sauce on top, and turn meatballs so they are fully coated in sauce.

5 Place pan in air fryer basket and cook 2 more minutes. When done, the meatballs will be browned and have an internal temperature of at least 165°F. Garnish with sesame seeds and green onion before serving.

PER SERVING

CALORIES: 179 | FAT: 8g | SODIUM: 986mg | CARBOHYDRATES: 7g | FIBER: 0g | SUGAR: 3g | PROTEIN: 19g

Cajun Corn Ribs

This fun appetizer is sure to spark conversation. Though they aren't actually ribs, these toasty, piquant corn wedges get their name from their resemblance to ribs after cooking. They're perfect for summer gatherings and barbecues, and they take less than 25 minutes to prep and cook. The Cajun seasoning adds the perfect spice level to challenge the natural sweetness of the corn and makes this otherwise simple vegetable a unique part of the party table.

Hands-On Time: 10 minutes
Cook Time: 13 minutes

Serves 8

- 4 medium ears corn, husks and silk removed
- 2 tablespoons salted butter, melted
- 1 tablespoon Cajun seasoning
- ¼ teaspoon salt

1 Preheat air fryer to 400°F. Place corn on a large plate and microwave 1 minute to soften cobs. Quarter each ear of corn by cutting it in half lengthwise, then cutting each half in half lengthwise again.

2 Brush butter over corn and sprinkle generously with Cajun seasoning and salt. Place corn in air fryer basket and cook 12 minutes, turning halfway through cooking. When done, corn will be tender and a kernel will easily pop when pressure is applied. Serve warm.

PER SERVING

CALORIES: 69 | FAT: 3g | SODIUM: 193mg | CARBOHYDRATES: 10g | FIBER: 1g | SUGAR: 3g | PROTEIN: 2g

Nacho Basket

Baked nachos have a unique flavor that makes them even more irresistible. The warm chips are revitalized, and the hot bubbling cheese makes them an instant comfort food. Feel free to add your favorite toppings to these game-day favorites, like sour cream and guacamole. You can even eat them right out of the foil for easy cleanup. Be sure to keep the foil out of the air fryer while it preheats. Without food to weigh the foil down, it may blow into the heating element of the machine and cause a fire hazard.

Hands-On Time: 5 minutes
Cook Time: 5 minutes

Serves 4

48 corn tortilla chips
½ cup nacho-style Cheddar cheese sauce
⅓ cup jarred sliced black olives
½ cup diced Roma tomatoes
¼ cup jarred sliced jalapeños

1 Preheat air fryer to 350°F. Cut a sheet of aluminum foil to fit bottom of air fryer basket. Place foil on a work surface.

2 Place chips on foil in an even layer. Pour cheese over chips, coating as well as possible. Carefully transfer nachos on foil to air fryer basket.

3 Cook 5 minutes, until chips are warmed and cheese is heated and bubbling. Top with olives, tomatoes, and jalapeños. Serve warm.

PER SERVING

CALORIES: 259 | FAT: 13g | SODIUM: 532mg | CARBOHYDRATES: 37g | FIBER: 3g | SUGAR: 2g | PROTEIN: 4g

Puff Pastry Cocktail Sausage Rolls

These poppable sausage rolls elevate mini cocktail sausages. Surrounded by golden brown puff pastry, this crowd favorite is a great appetizer that all ages will enjoy. The buttery puff pastry and savory sausage make an excellent pair in this elegant-looking appetizer that comes together in just over 20 minutes.

Hands-On Time: 10 minutes
Cook Time: 12 minutes

Yields 18

1 (13.2-ounce) package puff pastry, thawed
18 (0.3-ounce) fully cooked mini cocktail sausages
1 large egg, whisked
1 tablespoon sesame seeds

WHY THE HOLES?
Poking holes into the surface of dough is called docking, and its purpose is to prevent excess puffing while cooking. This method is common when working with puff pastry; it keeps the pastry from becoming distorted and too flaky. In the case of these sausage rolls, that means the pastry looks neater and adheres better to the meat.

1 Preheat air fryer to 375°F. On a clean work surface, unroll puff pastry and use a fork to dock crust. Cut pastry into 3" × 3" squares.

2 Place each square on work surface so that one corner points toward you like a diamond. Place a sausage in center of 1 pastry square vertically. Fold left and right corners over sausage and pinch to close, meeting in middle over center of sausage. Top and bottom sections of puff pastry will be open and sausage will slightly peak out on top and bottom. Repeat with remaining pastry and sausages.

3 Brush sausage rolls lightly with whisked egg, then turn them seam-side down to brush the smooth sides with egg wash and sprinkle lightly with sesame seeds.

4 Keeping rolls seam-side down, place in air fryer basket and cook 12 minutes, turning when 4 minutes of cooking time remain. When done, puff pastry will be browned and sausages will be heated through. Serve warm.

PER SERVING (SERVING SIZE: 3 ROLLS)

CALORIES: 324 | FAT: 23g | SODIUM: 479mg | CARBOHYDRATES: 21g | FIBER: 0g | SUGAR: 1g | PROTEIN: 7g

4

Side Dishes

After deciding what to serve for your main course, the most important question is always, "What sides will go with it?" Whether you're having an elegant dinner party or a casual supper, side dishes are essential in rounding out your meal. However, finding the time and kitchen space to have multiple dishes cooking at once can be a challenge, and you can easily end up with side dishes that aren't started by the time the entrée is done. Your air fryer is forever ready to tackle that challenge with ease, whipping up delicious side dishes in no time. From Chili Lime Elotes to Crispy Lemon Broccoli, this chapter is full of savory pairings that will add the perfect finishing touch to your meal.

Garlic Bread

This quick and easy side dish makes the perfect complement for all of your favorite Italian-style entrées. With its savory combination of butter, seasonings, and cheese, every mouthful will leave you craving another.

Hands-On Time: 5 minutes
Cook Time: 5 minutes

Yields 8

½ cup freshly grated
　　Parmesan cheese
¼ cup salted butter, softened
1 tablespoon mayonnaise
2 cloves garlic, peeled and
　　finely minced
¼ teaspoon dried oregano
8 (1") slices Italian bread
2 tablespoons fresh parsley,
　　finely chopped

FREEZER-FRIENDLY
Make an extra batch of Garlic Bread and freeze it to use as a last-minute meal addition whenever the need arises. To freeze, follow steps 1 and 2 of this recipe. Then, instead of baking, place slices on a baking sheet and par-freeze for 3 hours. Next, transfer to a freezer-safe sealable bag. To heat, place frozen slices in air fryer basket and bake at 350°F for 7 minutes, until golden brown.

1　Preheat air fryer to 350°F.

2　In a small bowl, mix Parmesan, butter, mayonnaise, garlic, and oregano until well combined. Spread about 1 tablespoon of mixture on each slice of bread in an even layer.

3　Place slices in air fryer basket, working in batches as necessary. Bake 5 minutes, until tops are golden brown and bubbling. Garnish with parsley. Serve warm. Store leftovers in an airtight container for up to 2 days.

PER SERVING (SERVING SIZE: 1 SLICE)

CALORIES: 144 | FAT: 9g | SODIUM: 292mg | CARBOHYDRATES: 11g | FIBER: 1g | SUGAR: 0g | PROTEIN: 4g

Roasted Edamame

This side dish comes together quickly and is full of flavor. The baby soybeans emerge from their pods with a satisfying snap that makes them fun to eat. Enjoy this dish alongside a loaded rice bowl or grilled meats.

Hands-On Time: 5 minutes
Cook Time: 15 minutes

Serves 4

2 tablespoons olive oil
1 tablespoon soy sauce
½ teaspoon garlic salt
¼ teaspoon ground ginger
8 ounces edamame in pods

1   Preheat air fryer to 375°F. In a medium bowl, whisk together olive oil, soy sauce, garlic salt, and ginger.

2   Toss edamame in mixture until well coated. Place edamame in air fryer basket and cook 15 minutes, shaking basket twice during cooking. When done, edamame will be tender and lightly browned. Serve warm.

PER SERVING

CALORIES: 130 | FAT: 9g | SODIUM: 464mg | CARBOHYDRATES: 8g | FIBER: 2g | SUGAR: 2g | PROTEIN: 6g

Easy Fried Plantains

Plantains may look similar to bananas, but these thicker and starchier fruits have a flavor profile all their own. Frying brings out their natural sweetness and adds a delightful crispiness. Be sure to use very ripe plantains for the best results.

Hands-On Time: 5 minutes
Cook Time: 12 minutes

Serves 4

2 large ripe plantains, cut into ¼"-thick diagonal slices
1 tablespoon coconut oil, melted
¼ teaspoon salt

1   Preheat air fryer to 400°F.

2   Lightly brush plantain slices with oil, then place in air fryer basket. Cook 12 minutes, turning halfway through cooking time. Plantains will be caramelized and tender when done. Sprinkle with salt and serve warm.

PER SERVING

CALORIES: 160 | FAT: 3g | SODIUM: 149mg | CARBOHYDRATES: 34g | FIBER: 2g | SUGAR: 16g | PROTEIN: 1g

Summer Vegetable Medley

Take full advantage of summer's freshest vegetables by creating a bright blend to serve alongside your meals. This medley can even be made in bulk and frozen.

Hands-On Time: 10 minutes
Cook Time: 10 minutes

Serves 4

1 medium zucchini, cut into ½"-thick slices

1 medium yellow summer squash, cut into ½"-thick slices

4 ounces cremini mushrooms (also called baby bellas), halved

1 cup small broccoli florets

2 tablespoons olive oil

½ teaspoon salt

½ teaspoon garlic powder

½ teaspoon dried oregano

¼ teaspoon ground black pepper

⅛ teaspoon crushed red pepper flakes

1 Preheat air fryer to 350°F. Place zucchini, squash, mushrooms, and broccoli in a large bowl. Drizzle olive oil over vegetables and sprinkle with salt, garlic powder, oregano, black pepper, and red pepper flakes, then toss to coat.

2 Scrape coated vegetables into a 6" round baking pan, then place in air fryer basket. Cook 10 minutes, stirring twice during cooking time. When done, vegetables will be tender. Serve warm.

PER SERVING

CALORIES: 90 | FAT: 7g | SODIUM: 304mg | CARBOHYDRATES: 6g | FIBER: 2g | SUGAR: 3g | PROTEIN: 3g

FREEZER-FRIENDLY

If you're prepping this dish to freeze, reduce the cook time by 5 minutes. This will ensure that your vegetables do not overcook when you reheat them. Parcooking (partially cooking) will help remove some of the excess moisture from the vegetables and reduce ice crystal formation during freezing. To reheat from frozen, preheat the air fryer to 300°F and cook in a greased baking dish for 15 minutes, until warmed.

Battered Potato Wedges

Crispy on the outside and perfectly tender within, these potato wedges are an excellent way to combat your French fry cravings with a more substantial and deliciously seasoned alternative. They go well alongside pork chops and make a great companion for Hot Italian Wraps (Chapter 6).

Hands-On Time: 10 minutes
Cook Time: 20 minutes

Serves 4

1 large egg
2 tablespoons whole milk
4 medium russet potatoes, scrubbed and cut into ¼" wedges
1 cup all-purpose flour
1 teaspoon salt
½ teaspoon ground black pepper
½ teaspoon ground paprika
¼ teaspoon garlic powder
¼ teaspoon onion powder

HOW TO CUT POTATO WEDGES

To cut wedges, begin by slicing a potato in half lengthwise. Place potatoes cut-side down and cut each half lengthwise for four even pieces total. With each cut side facing up, slice each potato quarter lengthwise into four even pieces for a total of eight potato wedges per potato.

1. Preheat air fryer to 350°F. In a large bowl, whisk together egg and milk until well combined. Place potato wedges in mixture.

2. Place flour in a large sealable bag and add salt, pepper, paprika, garlic powder, and onion powder. Close bag and shake to combine.

3. Allow excess egg to drip off potatoes, and place ⅓ of the potato wedges in flour mixture. Seal bag and toss to coat wedges. Repeat with remaining potato wedges until all are coated, placing coated wedges on a large plate while preparing remaining wedges.

4. Lightly spray wedges with cooking spray and place them in air fryer basket. Cook 20 minutes, shaking basket three times during cooking time. When done, wedges will be golden brown and crispy on the outside and insides will be tender. Serve warm.

PER SERVING

CALORIES: 276 | FAT: 2g | SODIUM: 481mg | CARBOHYDRATES: 56g | FIBER: 5g | SUGAR: 2g | PROTEIN: 9g

Orange Ginger Green Beans

Avoid green bean burnout by adding in the zippiest flavors. The ginger-citrus combination in this recipe makes for *the* most satisfying green beans.

Hands-On Time: 5 minutes
Cook Time: 10 minutes

Serves 4

12 ounces green beans, ends trimmed
1 tablespoon olive oil
2 tablespoons finely minced garlic
2 teaspoons grated fresh ginger
½ teaspoon salt
1 tablespoon orange zest
2 tablespoons salted butter, cut into ⅛"-thick slices

1 Preheat air fryer to 375°F. Place green beans in a 6" round baking pan. Drizzle with olive oil, then evenly sprinkle with garlic, ginger, salt, and orange zest.

2 Place butter on top of green beans. Place in air fryer basket and cook 10 minutes, shaking basket two times during cooking. When done, green beans will be tender. Serve warm.

PER SERVING

CALORIES: 114 | FAT: 9g | SODIUM: 341mg | CARBOHYDRATES: 8g | FIBER: 3g | SUGAR: 3g | PROTEIN: 2g

Crispy Parmesan Asparagus

Parmesan makes an excellent pairing for asparagus spears, elevating their flavor and transforming them into a dish your family will love.

Hands-On Time: 5 minutes
Cook Time: 8 minutes

Serves 4

1 pound asparagus, ends trimmed and cut into 3"-long pieces
2 tablespoons salted butter, melted
2 cloves garlic, peeled and finely minced
½ cup grated Parmesan cheese
¼ cup plain panko
½ teaspoon salt
¼ teaspoon ground black pepper

1 Preheat air fryer to 400°F. Place asparagus in a 6" round baking pan in a single layer, working in batches if needed.

2 Drizzle butter over asparagus, then sprinkle evenly with garlic, Parmesan, panko, salt, and pepper.

3 Place pan in air fryer basket and cook 8 minutes, until asparagus is tender and panko are browned. Serve warm.

PER SERVING

CALORIES: 143 | FAT: 9g | SODIUM: 576mg | CARBOHYDRATES: 10g | FIBER: 1g | SUGAR: 1g | PROTEIN: 6g

Parmesan Zucchini Chips

Roasting upgrades zucchini's flavor, and Parmesan is a wonderful complement for it. These golden brown and crispy chips are a light, nutrient-rich side for any protein-heavy meal.

Hands-On Time: 15 minutes
Cook Time: 8 minutes

Serves 4

2 medium zucchini, sliced with a mandoline into ⅛"-thick rounds
½ teaspoon salt
1 tablespoon olive oil
½ cup grated Parmesan cheese
¼ teaspoon paprika
¼ teaspoon garlic salt

1 Preheat air fryer to 400°F. Place zucchini in a single layer on a clean kitchen towel and sprinkle with salt. Allow to sit 10 minutes to draw out excess water—droplets will appear on top of slices.

2 Gently pat slices dry with a paper towel and place them in a large bowl. Drizzle with olive oil. Sprinkle in Parmesan, paprika, and garlic salt, and gently toss to coat.

3 Place zucchini in air fryer basket in a single layer, working in batches as needed. Cook 8 minutes, turning halfway through. When done, chips will be lightly browned. Place cooked chips on a paper towel on a cooling rack to cool at least 10 minutes before serving.

PER SERVING

CALORIES: 99 | FAT: 6g | SODIUM: 646mg | CARBOHYDRATES: 5g | FIBER: 1g | SUGAR: 2g | PROTEIN: 5g

Chili Lime Elotes

Inspired by the Mexican-style street food, these elotes build on the sweet and earthy flavor of corn with a bright and subtly spicy blend of seasonings. Don't forget the cotija cheese! It's the perfect creamy, salty finishing touch for these cobs.

Hands-On Time: 5 minutes
Cook Time: 15 minutes

Serves 4

4 medium ears corn, husks and silk removed
¼ cup salted butter, melted
1 teaspoon chili powder
Zest and juice of 2 small limes, zest divided
½ teaspoon salt
¼ teaspoon ground black pepper
¼ cup mayonnaise
¼ cup sour cream
½ cup crumbled cotija cheese
3 tablespoons chopped fresh cilantro

1 Preheat air fryer to 380°F. Brush each ear of corn all over with butter.

2 Evenly sprinkle corn with chili powder and 1 tablespoon lime zest, then with salt and pepper. Place corn in air fryer basket and cook 15 minutes, turning ⅔ of the way through cooking time. When done, corn will be tender.

3 In a small bowl, make sauce by whisking together mayonnaise, sour cream, lime juice, and remaining lime zest. Generously brush each corn cob all over with sauce, then sprinkle with cheese and cilantro. Serve warm.

PER SERVING

CALORIES: 369 | FAT: 29g | SODIUM: 720mg | CARBOHYDRATES: 22g | FIBER: 3g | SUGAR: 7g | PROTEIN: 7g

Cheddar Chive Drop Biscuits

Warm, buttery biscuits pair perfectly with almost everything, and they only get better when loaded up with herbs and flavorings. Get ready to indulge in some of the easiest, most flavor-packed drop biscuits ever.

Hands-On Time: 5 minutes
Cook Time: 12 minutes

Yields 8

2 cups plus 2 tablespoons self-rising flour, divided
4 tablespoons salted butter, frozen
¾ cup buttermilk
¾ cup shredded sharp Cheddar cheese
1 tablespoon chopped fresh chives

1 Preheat air fryer to 400°F. Cut a piece of parchment paper to fit air fryer basket.

2 Place 2 cups flour in a large bowl. Grate butter into bowl and use a wooden spoon to mix well. Pour in buttermilk and mix until a soft dough forms.

3 Place Cheddar and chives into a small bowl and add remaining 2 tablespoons flour. Toss to coat, then fold into dough.

4 Place parchment in air fryer basket. Scoop ¼ cup dough onto parchment. Repeat with remaining dough, leaving 2" of space between scoops. Working in batches as needed, cook 12 minutes, until golden brown and firm. Let cool 5 minutes before serving.

PER SERVING (SERVING SIZE: 1 BISCUIT)

CALORIES: 225 | FAT: 9g | SODIUM: 533mg | CARBOHYDRATES: 26g | FIBER: 1g | SUGAR: 1g | PROTEIN: 7g

Smoky Sweet Potato Fries

Smoked paprika gives this dish not only color but also a great deep, smoky flavor. Chipotle chili powder helps reinforce these flavors and offers a delicious juxtaposition that truly takes these fries to the next level.

Hands-On Time: 5 minutes
Cook Time: 10 minutes

Serves 4

2 large sweet potatoes, trimmed and sliced into ⅛" × ½" × 4" matchsticks
2 tablespoons olive oil
1 teaspoon smoked paprika
½ teaspoon salt
¼ teaspoon garlic salt
¼ teaspoon chipotle chili powder

1 Preheat air fryer to 400°F. Place sweet potatoes in a large bowl and drizzle with olive oil. Sprinkle with paprika, salt, garlic salt, and chili powder. Toss to coat evenly.

2 Place fries in air fryer basket and cook 10 minutes, shaking basket twice during cooking. When done, fries will be tender and browned. Serve warm.

PER SERVING

CALORIES: 142 | FAT: 7g | SODIUM: 450mg | CARBOHYDRATES: 19g | FIBER: 3g | SUGAR: 6g | PROTEIN: 2g

Easy Roasted Acorn Squash

Similar to butternut squash, this nutrient-rich vegetable has a mildly sweet, nutty flavor and a tender texture when roasted. It makes a wonderful side dish for everything from pork chops to roast chicken, creating a balanced, hearty meal.

Hands-On Time: 5 minutes
Cook Time: 15 minutes

Serves 4

1 (2-pound) acorn squash, halved and seeded
2 tablespoons olive oil
½ teaspoon salt
¼ teaspoon crushed red pepper flakes
¼ teaspoon ground black pepper

1 Preheat air fryer to 400°F. Brush inside of each half of acorn squash with olive oil and sprinkle with salt, red pepper flakes, and black pepper.

2 Place squash halves in air fryer basket and cook 15 minutes. When done, squash will be browned on top and tender. Serve warm.

PER SERVING

CALORIES: 125 | FAT: 7g | SODIUM: 295mg | CARBOHYDRATES: 17g | FIBER: 3g | SUGAR: 0g | PROTEIN: 1g

Seasoned Curly Fries

No one can resist the fun and flavor that come from perfectly crisp curly fries, and they're much easier to make at home than you might think. The key is to coat them in flour and make sure they cook up with plenty of flavor. Switch up the seasoning to match your taste preference, or give this simple blend a try.

Hands-On Time: 10 minutes
Cook Time: 12 minutes

Serves 4

3 large russet potatoes, peeled
3 tablespoons vegetable oil
¼ cup all-purpose flour
¾ teaspoon seasoned salt
½ teaspoon paprika
½ teaspoon garlic powder
¼ teaspoon ground black pepper

1 Spiralize each potato using a curly fry blade attachment (12mm) or the largest available noodle blade.

2 Preheat air fryer to 400°F. Use kitchen shears to cut curly fries into 6"-long pieces, and place them in a large bowl. Drizzle with oil.

3 In a small bowl, whisk together flour, seasoned salt, paprika, garlic powder, and pepper. Sprinkle on top of curly fries and toss to coat evenly.

4 Place fries in air fryer basket and cook 12 minutes, shaking basket two or three times during cooking. When done, fries will be golden brown and crisp. If any fries begin to look done early, carefully transfer them onto a paper towel–lined plate while continuing to cook remaining fries. Serve warm.

PER SERVING

CALORIES: 232 | FAT: 10g | SODIUM: 290mg | CARBOHYDRATES: 32g | FIBER: 2g | SUGAR: 2g | PROTEIN: 3g

Cheesy Roasted Cauliflower

This roasted cauliflower develops a light caramelization in the air fryer, which the added cheese only enhances. Cheesy cauliflower can be enjoyed on its own as a vegetarian meal, but it also makes a great side for hearty meat-based entrées too. If you don't typically love cauliflower, this recipe is a must-try that might just change your mind.

Hands-On Time: 5 minutes
Cook Time: 15 minutes

Serves 4

- 1 medium head cauliflower, leaves removed
- 2 tablespoons salted butter, melted
- 2 tablespoons mayonnaise
- 2 teaspoons Italian seasoning
- ½ teaspoon garlic salt
- ¼ teaspoon ground black pepper
- ¼ cup grated Parmesan cheese
- ½ cup shredded sharp Cheddar cheese
- ½ cup shredded mozzarella cheese

1 Preheat air fryer to 350°F. Spray a 6" pan with cooking spray and place cauliflower head inside pan.

2 In a small bowl, mix butter, mayonnaise, Italian seasoning, garlic salt, pepper, and Parmesan. Brush mixture evenly all over cauliflower.

3 Sprinkle Cheddar and mozzarella on top of cauliflower and gently press cheese into butter mixture to ensure it sticks. Place pan in air fryer basket and cook 15 minutes, until cheese is melted and cauliflower is tender. Serve warm.

PER SERVING

CALORIES: 250 | FAT: 18g | SODIUM: 655mg | CARBOHYDRATES: 9g | FIBER: 3g | SUGAR: 3g | PROTEIN: 11g

Roasted Cherry Tomatoes

Roasting tomatoes brings out their natural sweetness and magnifies their flavor. These roasted cherry tomatoes will brighten any dish. They're a tasty side dish on their own, and they can also be used to liven up your favorite pasta dishes or enjoyed on top of toasted Italian bread.

Hands-On Time: 5 minutes
Cook Time: 10 minutes

Serves 4

2 cups cherry tomatoes
2 tablespoons olive oil
1 teaspoon Italian seasoning
¼ teaspoon salt
3 cloves garlic, peeled
2 fresh basil leaves, thinly
   sliced

GARLIC

Minced and chopped garlic burns easily under the forced fan heat of an air fryer when it's not layered underneath other ingredients. This recipe leaves the cloves whole to infuse flavor without risking small, burned pieces among the tomatoes. You may choose to remove the garlic before eating or mash it up and mix it in. Alternatively, you can spread the softened garlic on a toasted baguette or Italian bread and top with the roasted tomatoes.

1   Preheat air fryer to 380°F. Place tomatoes in a 6" round baking pan and drizzle with olive oil.

2   Sprinkle Italian seasoning and salt on top of tomatoes and gently stir to coat. Place whole cloves of garlic in pan among tomatoes.

3   Place pan in air fryer basket and cook 10 minutes, stirring halfway through cooking. When done, tomatoes will be darker red and will have broken down and softened.

4   Remove garlic from pan. Top tomatoes with sliced basil and serve.

PER SERVING

CALORIES: 76 | FAT: 7g | SODIUM: 149mg | CARBOHYDRATES: 4g | FIBER: 1g | SUGAR: 2g | PROTEIN: 1g

Honey Butter Corn

This no-fuss recipe uses just a handful of simple ingredients for an easy side dish. Whether you're eating pork chops or chicken, this sweet, buttery corn dish is sure to liven up your plate.

Hands-On Time: 5 minutes
Cook Time: 12 minutes

Serves 4

2 cups frozen corn
3 tablespoons salted butter, melted
2 tablespoons honey
½ teaspoon salt
¼ teaspoon ground black pepper

1   Preheat air fryer to 370°F. Mix all ingredients in a 6" round baking pan until well combined.

2   Place pan in air fryer basket and cook 12 minutes, stirring three times during cooking. When done, corn will be tender. Serve warm.

PER SERVING

CALORIES: 168 | **FAT:** 9g | **SODIUM:** 361mg | **CARBOHYDRATES:** 23g | **FIBER:** 1g | **SUGAR:** 10g | **PROTEIN:** 2g

Twenty-Minute Dinner Rolls

Fluffy dinner rolls are a great comfort food but can be time-consuming to make completely from scratch. This recipe uses premade bread dough for a shortcut version of those delicious browned and buttered rolls everyone loves so much.

Hands-On Time: 10 minutes
Cook Time: 12 minutes

Serves 8

1 pound frozen bread dough, defrosted
1 large egg, whisked
3 tablespoons salted butter, melted

1   Preheat air fryer to 350°F. Cut a piece of parchment to fit air fryer basket and set aside.

2   Cut dough into 8 even pieces, roll each into a ball, and gently flatten tops. Lightly brush each with egg, and place on parchment in air fryer basket. Bake 12 minutes, until rolls are golden brown. Brush rolls with butter and serve warm.

PER SERVING

CALORIES: 183 | **FAT:** 6g | **SODIUM:** 315mg | **CARBOHYDRATES:** 27g | **FIBER:** 1g | **SUGAR:** 1g | **PROTEIN:** 4g

Maple Normandy Vegetables

Maple and rosemary may seem like an unlikely duo, but they actually complement each other in a variety of dishes. Rosemary's earthy flavor and maple syrup's sweetness elevate this simple frozen vegetable mix. The vegetables turn out tender and buttery, with a hint of roasted char on the edges.

Hands-On Time: 5 minutes
Cook Time: 15 minutes

Serves 4

- 2 cups Normandy-blend frozen vegetables
- 2 tablespoons pure maple syrup
- 2 teaspoons dried rosemary
- ½ teaspoon salt
- ¼ teaspoon ground black pepper
- 2 tablespoons salted butter, cut into ⅛"-thick slices

1 Preheat air fryer to 400°F. Spray a 6" round baking pan with cooking spray.

2 Place frozen vegetables in baking pan and drizzle with maple syrup. Add rosemary, salt, and pepper to pan and gently toss to coat. Top with sliced butter.

3 Place pan in air fryer basket and cook 15 minutes, stirring twice during cooking. When done, vegetables will be fork-tender. Serve warm.

PER SERVING

CALORIES: 92 | FAT: 5g | SODIUM: 347mg | CARBOHYDRATES: 10g | FIBER: 2g | SUGAR: 7g | PROTEIN: 1g

Crispy Lemon Broccoli

This is the perfect cruciferous dish and can accompany a wide range of entrées. Whether you're enjoying chicken or a vegetable bowl, this bright and flavorful side dish adds a pop of color—and dose of vitamin K. Serve with lemon slices on the side for an even more colorful presentation.

Hands-On Time: 5 minutes
Cook Time: 10 minutes

Serves 4

2 cups fresh broccoli florets
2 tablespoons olive oil
Zest and juice of ½ medium lemon
½ teaspoon garlic salt
¼ teaspoon ground black pepper

SWAP FOR FROZEN

Swap the fresh florets in this recipe for frozen broccoli. Add 3–4 minutes of cook time to let broccoli become perfectly tender and browned.

1 Preheat air fryer to 350°F.

2 Place broccoli in a large bowl and drizzle with olive oil, lemon juice, lemon zest, garlic salt, and pepper.

3 Place broccoli in air fryer basket and cook 10 minutes, shaking basket halfway through cooking. When done, broccoli will be crispy and lightly browned at the edges and stalks will be tender. Serve warm.

PER SERVING

CALORIES: 76 | FAT: 7g | SODIUM: 260mg | CARBOHYDRATES: 4g | FIBER: 1g | SUGAR: 1g | PROTEIN: 1g

Buttermilk Corn Bread Bites

These bites are an excellent side dish for hearty meals. They can be whipped up in less than 20 minutes and have a delicious tangy flavor that goes with many different entrées. Their crunchy exterior is perfect for enjoying alongside stew or chili. Feel free to add a spoonful of finely chopped onions to the mix if you're a fan of traditional hush puppies.

Hands-On Time: 5 minutes
Cook Time: 12 minutes

Yields 8

1 (8.5-ounce) package Jiffy corn muffin mix
½ cup all-purpose flour
⅓ cup buttermilk
1 large egg
3 tablespoons vegetable oil

1   Preheat air fryer to 400°F.

2   In a large bowl, mix corn muffin mix, flour, buttermilk, and egg until a mostly smooth, thick batter forms.

3   Scoop up 2 tablespoons of batter and roll into a ball. Brush lightly with vegetable oil and place in air fryer basket, leaving 1" space between balls. Repeat with remaining mixture.

4   Cook 12 minutes, turning halfway through cooking. When done, balls will be golden brown and firm and a toothpick inserted will come out mostly clean. Allow 5 minutes to cool before serving.

PER SERVING (SERVING SIZE: 2 BITES)

CALORIES: 216 | FAT: 9g | SODIUM: 289mg | CARBOHYDRATES: 28g | FIBER: 0g | SUGAR: 6g | PROTEIN: 4g

Easy Loaded Potatoes

Potatoes are a versatile ingredient, but cooking them from scratch can be time-consuming. This recipe is perfect for those short on time who love a baked potato but don't want to spend nearly an hour cooking it in the oven. Using frozen potatoes and savory toppings gives you all the flavor without the fuss.

Hands-On Time: 5 minutes
Cook Time: 20 minutes

Serves 4

2 cups frozen diced potatoes
½ teaspoon salt
½ teaspoon paprika
¼ teaspoon ground black pepper
¼ cup crumbled cooked bacon
½ cup shredded mild Cheddar cheese
2 tablespoons sour cream
1 medium green onion, thinly sliced

1 Preheat air fryer to 400°F. Place potatoes in a 6" round baking pan and spray lightly with olive oil spray.

2 Sprinkle potatoes with salt, paprika, and pepper, and toss to coat. Place pan in air fryer basket and cook 15 minutes, shaking once during cooking.

3 Remove basket from air fryer and, leaving potatoes in basket, carefully sprinkle with crumbled bacon and top with shredded cheese. Return to air fryer and cook 5 more minutes, until cheese is melted. Top with sour cream and green onion, then serve.

PER SERVING

CALORIES: 224 | FAT: 10g | SODIUM: 660mg | CARBOHYDRATES: 20g | FIBER: 2g | SUGAR: 0g | PROTEIN: 11g

Carrot Fries

This dish is an excellent way to bring some excitement to your daily serving of vegetables. Air frying carrots bring out their natural sugars, which caramelize and make a delicious balance of sweet and savory flavors. The most time-consuming part of this recipe is the chopping, and that can be done in advance to shorten your kitchen time before your meal—just store cut carrots in a sealable bag in the refrigerator until you're ready to use them.

Hands-On Time: 5 minutes
Cook Time: 20 minutes

Serves 4

1 pound carrots, peeled, ends removed
1 tablespoon olive oil
½ teaspoon salt
½ teaspoon smoked paprika
¼ teaspoon ground black pepper

1 Preheat air fryer to 400°F. On a clean work surface, cut carrots in half lengthwise, then cut each half into 3 fry-shaped pieces.

2 Drizzle olive oil over carrots and sprinkle with salt, paprika, and pepper. Place carrots in air fryer basket and cook 20 minutes, shaking basket twice during cooking. When done, carrots will have crispy edges and be fork-tender in center. Serve warm.

PER SERVING

CALORIES: 75 | FAT: 3g | SODIUM: 366mg | CARBOHYDRATES: 11g | FIBER: 3g | SUGAR: 5g | PROTEIN: 1g

5

Chicken Main Dishes

Chicken is great to have for protein-rich and inexpensive meals, but it can be tough to decide what to do with it, especially if you're serving it up often. Nobody wants to spend a ton of time in the kitchen trying to get it just right, and if you go a simple route, you can quickly fall into a pattern of uninspired, bland dishes. But this chapter is here to make sure that never happens again. With page after page of meals that are easy and still bursting with flavor, this chapter will help you fine-tune your meal rotation and satisfy your whole family's taste buds with recipes like Teriyaki Chicken Meatballs and Southern Dry-Rub Wings!

Honey Balsamic Chicken Wings

From the sweetness of the honey to the tanginess of the balsamic glaze and the warm ginger undertones throughout, these irresistible wings come together as a harmonious balance of flavors.

Hands-On Time: 5 minutes
Cook Time: 20 minutes

Serves 4

2 pounds chicken wings, drums and flats separated
½ teaspoon salt
¼ teaspoon ground black pepper
⅓ cup honey
2 tablespoons balsamic glaze
1 tablespoon soy sauce
⅛ teaspoon ground ginger

BALSAMIC GLAZE

Balsamic glaze is made when balsamic vinegar is reduced until it's a thick consistency similar to honey. It has a deep, sweet flavor that goes well with meat, vegetables, and even some desserts. You can usually find balsamic glaze in the condiment section at the grocery store.

1 Preheat air fryer to 350°F. Sprinkle wings evenly with salt and pepper. Place wings in air fryer basket and cook 15 minutes, flipping halfway through cooking.

2 To make sauce, in a small bowl, whisk together honey, balsamic glaze, soy sauce, and ginger until combined.

3 When wings have cooked 15 minutes, brush all over with sauce and adjust air fryer temperature to 400°F. Place wings back in air fryer for 2 minutes, then brush all over with another layer of sauce and cook another 3 minutes. When done, wings will be dark brown in color, with an internal temperature of at least 165°F. Serve warm.

PER SERVING

CALORIES: 562 | FAT: 29g | SODIUM: 684mg | CARBOHYDRATES: 31g | FIBER: 0g | SUGAR: 30g | PROTEIN: 43g

Teriyaki Chicken Meatballs

Ground chicken allows you the versatility to make everything from chicken burgers to chicken meatballs. This flavor-packed and juicy entrée combines garlic, ginger, and teriyaki sauce to create a savory taste experience that pairs wonderfully with rice. If you can't find ground chicken at your grocery store, feel free to swap in ground turkey.

Hands-On Time: 10 minutes
Cook Time: 10 minutes

Yields 16

1 pound ground chicken breast
½ cup plain panko
1 large egg
½ teaspoon salt
½ teaspoon garlic powder
½ teaspoon ground ginger
¼ teaspoon ground black pepper
1 cup teriyaki sauce
1 tablespoon water
1 tablespoon cornstarch
2 medium green onions, thinly sliced

1 Preheat air fryer to 370°F. In a large bowl, mix ground chicken, panko, egg, salt, garlic powder, ginger, and pepper until well combined.

2 Separate mixture into 18 meatballs, about 2 tablespoons of mixture each. Place in air fryer and cook 8 minutes, shaking basket halfway through cooking. When done, meatballs will have an internal temperature of 165°F and be lightly browned and firm.

3 In a large bowl, whisk together teriyaki sauce, water, and cornstarch until well combined. Toss meatballs in teriyaki sauce. Place meatballs back in air fryer basket and cook 2 more minutes, until sauce becomes sticky and dark. Sprinkle green onions on top and serve warm.

PER SERVING (SERVING SIZE: 4 MEATBALLS)

CALORIES: 315 | FAT: 11g | SODIUM: 3,164mg | CARBOHYDRATES: 24g | FIBER: 0g | SUGAR: 11g | PROTEIN: 29g

Caprese Chicken

Caprese chicken is a wonderful blend of fresh and bold flavors. This recipe brings together rich and tangy balsamic, creamy mozzarella, and juicy fresh tomato for a delicious meal that comes together quickly.

Hands-On Time: 5 minutes
Cook Time: 12 minutes

Serves 4

- 2 tablespoons olive oil
- 1 tablespoon balsamic vinegar
- ½ tablespoon honey
- ½ teaspoon Dijon mustard
- 2 (6-ounce) boneless, skinless chicken breasts, cut in half lengthwise into thin cutlets
- 2 teaspoons Italian seasoning
- 1 teaspoon salt
- ¼ teaspoon ground black pepper
- 1 large beefsteak tomato, cut into ¼"-thick slices
- 4 ounces fresh mozzarella cheese, cut into ¼"-thick slices
- 4 leaves fresh basil, thinly sliced

1 Preheat air fryer to 360°F. In a small bowl, whisk together olive oil, balsamic vinegar, honey, and Dijon until well combined.

2 Sprinkle each piece of chicken all over with Italian seasoning, salt, and pepper, then generously brush olive oil mixture all over each piece of chicken. Place chicken in air fryer basket and cook 12 minutes, turning ⅔ of the way through cooking. When done, chicken will have an internal temperature of 165°F and juices will run clear.

3 Place a slice of tomato and a slice of mozzarella on each piece of chicken. Garnish with basil, and serve warm.

PER SERVING

CALORIES: 253 | FAT: 13g | SODIUM: 824mg | CARBOHYDRATES: 6g | FIBER: 0g | SUGAR: 3g | PROTEIN: 26g

Garlic Parmesan Chicken Tenderloins

Chicken tenderloins are a great addition to your weekly meal rotation. They are boneless, smaller cuts of meat that cook up quickly and are budget-friendly. This makes them perfect for busy weeknight dinners. This recipe adds a creamy cheese coating that seals in moisture, making these tenderloins an extra-juicy main dish.

Hands-On Time: 5 minutes
Cook Time: 12 minutes

Serves 4

- ⅓ cup mayonnaise
- 3 cloves garlic, peeled and finely minced
- 2 tablespoons grated Parmesan cheese
- 2 teaspoons lemon juice
- ⅛ teaspoon crushed red pepper flakes
- ⅛ teaspoon dried oregano
- ½ teaspoon salt
- ¼ teaspoon ground black pepper
- 1 pound chicken tenderloins

1 Preheat air fryer to 370°F. In a medium bowl, whisk together mayonnaise, garlic, Parmesan, lemon juice, red pepper flakes, and oregano until well combined.

2 Sprinkle salt and black pepper on chicken tenderloin pieces and brush each all over generously with mayonnaise mixture. Place tenderloins in air fryer basket and cook 12 minutes, turning once halfway through cooking. When done, tenderloins will be browned and have an internal temperature of at least 165°F. Serve warm.

PER SERVING

CALORIES: 212 | FAT: 14g | SODIUM: 533mg | CARBOHYDRATES: 1g | FIBER: 0g | SUGAR: 0g | PROTEIN: 17g

Southern Dry-Rub Wings

Wings are one of the best air fryer dishes for beginners. They open your eyes to how truly crispy chicken can get without using a deep fryer. These wings are seasoned simply, but you'll be amazed at how deeply golden brown they get while staying juicy inside. Serve with raw sliced vegetables and your favorite dipping sauce.

Hands-On Time: 5 minutes
Cook Time: 20 minutes

Serves 4

2 pounds chicken wings, flats and drums separated
1 teaspoon salt
1 teaspoon smoked paprika
½ teaspoon garlic powder
½ teaspoon dried oregano
¼ teaspoon onion powder
⅛ teaspoon dried thyme
⅛ teaspoon cayenne pepper

1 Preheat air fryer to 400°F. Place wings in a large bowl and pat with a paper towel to remove excess moisture.

2 In a small bowl, mix salt, paprika, garlic powder, oregano, onion powder, thyme, and cayenne until well combined. Sprinkle spice mixture on top of wings and toss to coat evenly.

3 Place wings in air fryer basket and cook 20 minutes, shaking basket three times during cooking. When done, wings will be browned and have an internal temperature of at least 165°F. Serve warm.

PER SERVING

CALORIES: 452 | FAT: 29g | SODIUM: 754mg | CARBOHYDRATES: 1g | FIBER: 0g | SUGAR: 0g | PROTEIN: 42g

Spicy Chicken Poppers

These poppers are perfect for meal prep because they're so simple and can be enjoyed with salad or on top of rice. They work equally well as a protein-rich snack that will leave you feeling satisfied, or as the centerpiece of a dinner that everyone will love. Each bite is juicy and full of cheese, vegetables, and a ton of flavor. Feel free to switch up the vegetables and cheese to cater to taste preferences and please those who like more or less spice.

Hands-On Time: 10 minutes
Cook Time: 15 minutes

Yields 20

- 1 pound ground chicken breast
- ½ medium green bell pepper, seeded and finely chopped
- ½ medium jalapeño, seeded and chopped
- ½ cup shredded pepper jack cheese
- 1 teaspoon salt
- ½ teaspoon ground cumin
- ½ teaspoon paprika
- ½ teaspoon chili powder
- ¼ teaspoon garlic salt

1 Preheat air fryer to 350°F. In a large bowl, combine all ingredients. Form 20 balls, 1½" across, and place them in a single layer in air fryer basket.

2 Spray balls lightly with cooking spray and cook 15 minutes, shaking basket twice during cooking. When done, poppers will be golden brown and have an internal temperature of at least 165°F. Serve warm.

PER SERVING (SERVING SIZE: 5 POPPERS)

CALORIES: 229 | FAT: 13g | SODIUM: 866mg | CARBOHYDRATES: 1g | FIBER: 1g | SUGAR: 1g | PROTEIN: 25g

Crispy Chicken Thighs

Bone-in chicken thighs are a flavorful cut of meat that makes for an easy dinner. If you typically buy boneless, skinless cuts, don't let bone-in thighs intimidate you: Cooking them with the bone adds lots of great flavor. The air fryer transforms them into a succulent and tender dish with an extra-crispy skin that will earn them a spot on your favorites list.

Hands-On Time: 5 minutes
Cook Time: 25 minutes

Serves 4

- 4 (6-ounce) bone-in, skin-on chicken thighs
- 1 tablespoon lemon zest
- 1 teaspoon paprika
- ½ teaspoon garlic powder
- ½ teaspoon salt
- ½ teaspoon dried thyme
- ¼ teaspoon ground black pepper
- ¼ teaspoon garlic salt

WHY COOK SKIN-SIDE DOWN?
Chicken thighs naturally have a lot of fat in the meat compared to breast pieces. During cooking, the fat drips downward. Cooking the thighs skin-side down initially allows the fat to coat the skin and gives it an extra-crisp texture.

1 Preheat air fryer to 370°F. Sprinkle chicken thighs evenly with lemon zest, paprika, garlic powder, salt, thyme, pepper, and garlic salt so that they're well coated on each side.

2 Place chicken thighs in air fryer basket, skin sides down, and cook 25 minutes, turning when 8 minutes of cooking time remain. When done, juices will run clear and internal temperature will be at least 165°F. Serve warm.

PER SERVING

CALORIES: 230 | FAT: 10g | SODIUM: 512mg | CARBOHYDRATES: 1g | FIBER: 0g | SUGAR: 0g | PROTEIN: 32g

Lemon Herb Drumsticks

In the oven, drumsticks can take upwards of 40 minutes to fully crisp, but the air fryer cooks them in a fraction of the time. .

Hands-On Time: 5 minutes
Cook Time: 25 minutes

Serves 4

1 tablespoon lemon pepper seasoning
1 teaspoon dried thyme
1 teaspoon dried basil
1 teaspoon dried oregano
½ teaspoon garlic powder
8 skin-on chicken drumsticks

1 Preheat air fryer to 350°F. In a small bowl, mix lemon pepper seasoning, thyme, basil, oregano, and garlic powder.

2 Pat drumsticks with a paper towel to remove excess moisture. Sprinkle seasoning mixture all over drumsticks and rub into skin until well coated. Place drumsticks in air fryer basket and cook 25 minutes, turning twice during cooking. When done, drumsticks will be golden and crispy and have an internal temperature of at least 165°F.

PER SERVING

CALORIES: 403 | FAT: 19g | SODIUM: 348mg | CARBOHYDRATES: 1g | FIBER: 0g | SUGAR: 0g | PROTEIN: 49g

Chicken Alfredo Pizza

Premade pizza crusts make this dinner a breeze. You can also try topping the pizza with broccolini for a pop of color.

Hands-On Time: 5 minutes
Cook Time: 10 minutes

Serves 4

4 (4") premade refrigerated pizza crusts
¾ cup Alfredo sauce
1 cup shredded mozzarella cheese
½ cup grated Parmesan cheese
1 cup finely diced cooked chicken breast
2 tablespoons chopped fresh parsley

1 Preheat air fryer to 370°F. Place pizza crusts on a work surface. Spread 3 tablespoons sauce on each crust, then sprinkle each with ¼ cup shredded mozzarella and 2 tablespoons Parmesan. Top each with ¼ cup chicken.

2 Working in batches as needed, place pizzas in air fryer basket and cook 10 minutes. When done, cheese will be browned and sauce will be bubbling. Garnish with fresh parsley, then serve warm.

PER SERVING

CALORIES: 398 | FAT: 17g | SODIUM: 1,271mg | CARBOHYDRATES: 33g | FIBER: 0g | SUGAR: 5g | PROTEIN: 25g

Italian Chicken

Everyone needs a go-to chicken recipe. Whether you're prepping a batch of it for weekday meals or simply need a quick option for wraps, pasta, and salad, this dish will cover all of your chicken needs. The chicken bouillon is the key ingredient—it infuses roasted flavor into the chicken without it needing to cook for an extended period of time.

Hands-On Time: 5 minutes
Cook Time: 12 minutes

Serves 8

2 teaspoons salt
2 teaspoons Italian seasoning
1 teaspoon powdered chicken bouillon
1 teaspoon garlic powder
1 teaspoon paprika
½ teaspoon ground black pepper
8 (3-ounce) boneless, skinless chicken breast cutlets
2 tablespoons olive oil

FREEZER-FRIENDLY

You can freeze the chicken in whole pieces or chop it for easy use. If you want to freeze the chicken shredded or diced, par-freezing it will prevent pieces from sticking together and allow you to grab smaller portions easily. Simply spread the shredded or diced chicken on a large baking sheet, freeze for 2 hours, and then transfer to a freezer-safe sealable bag. The best flavor lasts up to 2 months in the freezer.

1 Preheat air fryer to 370°F. In a small bowl, whisk together salt, Italian seasoning, chicken bouillon, garlic powder, paprika, and pepper until well combined.

2 Place chicken in a large bowl and drizzle with olive oil. Sprinkle spice mixture on top of chicken and toss to coat well. Place chicken in air fryer basket and cook 12 minutes, turning halfway through cooking. When done, chicken will be lightly browned and have an internal temperature of at least 165°F. Allow 5 minutes to cool before slicing and serving.

PER SERVING

CALORIES: 125 | FAT: 5g | SODIUM: 673mg | CARBOHYDRATES: 1g | FIBER: 0g | SUGAR: 0g | PROTEIN: 19g

Hot Honey–Glazed Chicken Thighs

If you're a fan of spicy glazes, this hot honey chicken is a must-try. Hot honey has the ideal balance of sweetness and subtle, spicy flavor and makes these thighs a meal to remember. In less than 30 minutes you can have a deliciously juicy dish on the table. Feel free to use boneless, skinless chicken thighs—just reduce the cooking time to 15 minutes.

Hands-On Time: 5 minutes
Cook Time: 20 minutes

Serves 4

- 1 teaspoon salt
- ½ teaspoon garlic powder
- ¼ teaspoon onion powder
- ¼ teaspoon smoked paprika
- ¼ teaspoon crushed red pepper flakes
- 2 pounds bone-in, skin-on chicken thighs
- 2 tablespoons salted butter, melted
- ½ cup hot honey

1 Preheat air fryer to 370°F. In a small bowl, mix salt, garlic powder, onion powder, paprika, and red pepper flakes. Sprinkle mixture evenly on all sides of chicken thighs, pressing some spices underneath chicken skin.

2 Lightly spray air fryer basket with nonstick cooking spray. Place chicken thighs in air fryer basket skin-side down. Cook 20 minutes, turning thighs skin-side up halfway through cooking time. When done, skin will be browned, internal temperature will be at least 165°F, and juices will run clear.

3 In a small bowl, whisk butter with honey. Generously brush each piece of chicken all over with butter mixture. Serve warm.

PER SERVING

CALORIES: 522 | FAT: 20g | SODIUM: 777mg | CARBOHYDRATES: 35g | FIBER: 0g | SUGAR: 35g | PROTEIN: 48g

Garlic Herb–Baked Chicken

Busy weeknights need simple meal solutions, and this recipe is sure to be your new go-to. Enjoy it as a main dish, or slice it up and use it as a protein boost in a pasta dish or salad. This recipe has a mix of herbs and spices with a hint of sweetness that gives the edges a deliciously caramelized flavor.

Hands-On Time: 10 minutes
Cook Time: 15 minutes

Serves 4

2 tablespoons olive oil
4 (6-ounce) chicken breasts, butterflied
1 tablespoon light brown sugar, packed
½ teaspoon garlic powder
½ teaspoon salt
¼ teaspoon smoked paprika
¼ teaspoon ground black pepper
¼ teaspoon dried thyme
¼ teaspoon dried oregano

1 Preheat air fryer to 370°F.

2 Drizzle olive oil onto each side of chicken pieces. In a small bowl, mix brown sugar, garlic powder, salt, paprika, pepper, thyme, and oregano until combined. Sprinkle mixture evenly onto all sides of chicken.

3 Place chicken in air fryer basket and cook 15 minutes, turning after 10 minutes. When done, chicken will be lightly browned and have an internal temperature of at least 165°F. Allow chicken to rest 5 minutes before slicing. Serve warm.

PER SERVING

CALORIES: 259 | FAT: 10g | SODIUM: 355mg | CARBOHYDRATES: 4g | FIBER: 0g | SUGAR: 3g | PROTEIN: 38g

WHY BUTTERFLY?

Butterflying chicken breasts before air frying is a great technique to ensure even cooking. Chicken breasts are often thick at the top and get smaller toward the end of the cut, and the thinner meat is more prone to dry out. Butterflying, or horizontally cutting the chicken breast evenly in half, cuts down on the cook time for the center so the rest of the piece can remain juicy.

Buffalo Ranch Chicken Tenderloins

Buffalo and ranch are a winning combination, especially when it comes to easy dinners. A ranch seasoning packet is an excellent way to add lots of flavor to your chicken quickly without grabbing lots of spices from the cabinet. The zesty seasoning adds a delicious tang alongside the spicy hot sauce. If spice isn't your thing, you can skip the hot sauce for a tasty but milder meal.

Hands-On Time: 10 minutes
Cook Time: 15 minutes

Serves 4

1 pound chicken tenderloins
1 tablespoon olive oil
1 (1-ounce) packet ranch
   seasoning
¼ teaspoon salt
⅛ teaspoon ground black
   pepper
1 cup hot sauce
¼ cup salted butter, melted

1   Preheat air fryer to 370°F. Place chicken in a large bowl and drizzle with olive oil. Sprinkle ranch seasoning, salt, and pepper on top of chicken and toss to coat.

2   Place tenderloins in air fryer basket. Cook 15 minutes, turning halfway through cooking. When done, tenders will be browned and have an internal temperature of at least 165°F.

3   In a clean large bowl, whisk together hot sauce and melted butter. Toss cooked chicken tenders in hot sauce mixture and serve.

PER SERVING

CALORIES: 224 | **FAT:** 14g | **SODIUM:** 2,688mg | **CARBOHYDRATES:** 4g | **FIBER:** 0g | **SUGAR:** 0g | **PROTEIN:** 16g

Mediterranean Chicken Burgers

Vegetables are at the forefront of these juicy burgers for a nutritious and flavorful weeknight meal option. They can even be prepped the night before to save time the day of. If you're a fan of feta cheese, you can add ½ cup crumbled feta to the mixture before cooking for a creamy and tangy twist. Serve alongside Smoky Sweet Potato Fries (Chapter 4) for a well-rounded meal.

Hands-On Time: 5 minutes
Cook Time: 12 minutes

Serves 4

1 pound ground chicken breast
1 cup loosely packed fresh baby spinach, chopped
¼ cup chopped red onion
½ medium red bell pepper, seeded and chopped
1 teaspoon salt
½ teaspoon cumin
¼ teaspoon dried oregano
¼ teaspoon ground black pepper
4 whole-wheat burger buns
1 large beefsteak tomato, cut into ¼"-thick slices
8 medium leaves Bibb lettuce

1 Preheat air fryer to 370°F.

2 In a medium bowl, mix ground chicken, spinach, onion, bell pepper, salt, cumin, oregano, and black pepper until well combined. Separate mixture into 4 even portions and shape into 5"-wide patties.

3 Spray air fryer basket with nonstick cooking spray and place patties in basket. Cook 12 minutes, turning halfway through cooking. When done, patties will have an internal temperature of at least 165°F and juices will run clear.

4 Place burgers on buns and top each with sliced tomato and lettuce, then serve.

PER SERVING

CALORIES: 341 | FAT: 11g | SODIUM: 2,152mg | CARBOHYDRATES: 32g | FIBER: 5g | SUGAR: 5g | PROTEIN: 28g

Jamaican Jerk Chicken Sandwiches

These easy chicken sandwiches are packed with flavor and make a great alternative to battered chicken sandwiches. A spicy jerk seasoning paste coats the chicken thighs and is balanced by a refreshing mango salsa. Walkerswood jerk seasoning was used to develop this recipe and provides a bold, authentic flavor for these sandwiches. You can usually find it in major grocery stores and online.

Hands-On Time: 5 minutes
Cook Time: 15 minutes

Serves 4

- 4 boneless, skinless chicken thighs
- 1 tablespoon mild jerk seasoning paste
- ½ teaspoon salt
- ¼ teaspoon ground black pepper
- 4 sweet Hawaiian-style burger buns
- ½ cup mango salsa

MANGO SALSA

Look for mango salsa that has mangos rather than tomatoes as the first ingredient. Mango-heavy salsas are usually lighter in color and have a stronger fruit flavor than those that are dark red and contain more tomatoes. Alternatively, you can use pineapple salsa or pineapple slices to top these sandwiches.

1 Preheat air fryer to 380°F. Place chicken thighs in a medium bowl and rub with seasoning paste until coated. Sprinkle salt and pepper evenly over each chicken thigh.

2 Lightly spray air fryer basket with cooking spray and place chicken thighs in air fryer basket. Cook 15 minutes, turning halfway through cooking. When done, thighs will be browned and have an internal temperature of at least 165°F.

3 Place each piece of chicken onto a bun and top with mango salsa. Serve warm.

PER SERVING

CALORIES: 425 | FAT: 19g | SODIUM: 732mg | CARBOHYDRATES: 28g | FIBER: 0g | SUGAR: 11g | PROTEIN: 31g

Salsa Chicken

Whether you shred and dice it for tacos or eat it alongside a serving of rice, this succulent chicken is as easy to make as it is delicious. Look for a chunky salsa to enjoy juicy bites of tomato with each moist piece of chicken. Feel free to switch things up by adding cheese and/or sour cream or replacing the tomato salsa with salsa verde.

Hands-On Time: 5 minutes
Cook Time: 18 minutes

Serves 4

- 4 (6-ounce) boneless, skinless chicken breasts
- 1 tablespoon olive oil
- 1 (1-ounce) packet mild taco seasoning
- 1 cup mild tomato salsa
- ½ cup drained and rinsed canned corn kernels

1 Preheat air fryer to 370°F. Brush chicken with olive oil, then sprinkle with taco seasoning on each side.

2 Working in batches as needed, place chicken in a 6" round baking pan. Top with salsa and corn. Place in air fryer basket and cook 18 minutes. When done, chicken will have an internal temperature of at least 165°F.

3 Carefully scoop chicken onto a large plate and spoon over sauce from pan. Serve warm.

PER SERVING

CALORIES: 267 | FAT: 7g | SODIUM: 1,064mg | CARBOHYDRATES: 11g | FIBER: 3g | SUGAR: 5g | PROTEIN: 38g

Barbecue Pineapple Chicken Kebabs

Pineapple and barbecue may seem like an unlikely duo, but once you taste the mix of smoky and sweet flavors, you'll be sold. These kebabs bring together delicious tender-crisp vegetables and juicy chicken. To further simplify meal time, you can even prepare and skewer everything early in the day. Just refrigerate, then pop the kebabs into the air fryer right before your meal.

Hands-On Time: 10 minutes
Cook Time: 10 minutes

Serves 4

- 1½ pounds boneless, skinless chicken breast, cut into 1" cubes
- ¾ cup barbecue sauce
- 1 teaspoon salt
- ¼ teaspoon ground black pepper
- 1 cup drained canned pineapple chunks
- 1 medium red bell pepper, seeded and cut into 1" chunks
- 1 medium green bell pepper, seeded and cut into 1" chunks
- 1 medium red onion, peeled and cut into 1" chunks

1 Preheat air fryer to 370°F. Place chicken in a medium bowl and toss with barbecue sauce, salt, and black pepper.

2 Arrange chicken pieces, pineapple chunks, and bell pepper and onion chunks on 6" metal kebab skewers in an alternating pattern until all ingredients are used. Place kebabs in the air fryer basket and cook 10 minutes, flipping halfway through cooking. When done, chicken will have an internal temperature of at least 165°F and vegetables will be slightly charred and tender. Serve warm.

PER SERVING

CALORIES: 333 | FAT: 4g | SODIUM: 1,199mg | CARBOHYDRATES: 35g | FIBER: 3g | SUGAR: 27g | PROTEIN: 40g

Pesto Chicken Tenders

While you're boiling a pot of pasta on the stove you can put the air fryer to work making these chicken tenderloins. These tasty tenderloins cook up quickly and require only four simple ingredients, making them one of the easiest go-to recipes.

Hands-On Time: 5 minutes
Cook Time: 15 minutes

Serves 4

1 pound chicken tenderloins
½ cup basil pesto
½ teaspoon salt
¼ teaspoon ground black pepper

1 Preheat air fryer to 370°F. Working in batches as needed, place tenderloins in a 6" round baking pan. Pour pesto over chicken and sprinkle with salt and pepper. Rotate chicken pieces to coat them with pesto on all sides.

2 Place pan with chicken in air fryer basket and cook 15 minutes, turning chicken halfway through cooking. When done, chicken will have an internal temperature of at least 165°F. Serve warm.

PER SERVING

CALORIES: 195 | **FAT:** 12g | **SODIUM:** 653mg | **CARBOHYDRATES:** 3g | **FIBER:** 1g | **SUGAR:** 1g | **PROTEIN:** 18g

Chicken-Fried Rice

This dish turns leftover rice and chicken (or store-bought rotisserie chicken) into an entirely new meal that's both simple and flavorful. You'll need cold precooked rice, so if you don't have leftovers, plan ahead and make a batch the night before so it has time to chill.

Hands-On Time: 5 minutes
Cook Time: 18 minutes

Serves 4

1½ cups diced cooked chicken breast
3 cups cold cooked white rice
1 cup frozen mixed carrots and peas
3 tablespoons soy sauce
2 teaspoons vegetable oil
2 tablespoons water
1 medium green onion, thinly sliced

1 Preheat air fryer to 370°F. Mix all ingredients except green onion in a large bowl until well combined.

2 Scrape mixture into a 6" round baking pan sprayed with nonstick cooking spray. Place pan in air fryer basket and cook 18 minutes, stirring twice during cooking.

3 When done, rice will be hot and vegetables will be tender. Serve warm, garnished with green onion.

PER SERVING

CALORIES: 314 | **FAT:** 4g | **SODIUM:** 752mg | **CARBOHYDRATES:** 45g | **FIBER:** 2g | **SUGAR:** 0g | **PROTEIN:** 22g

Easy Crispy Drumsticks

Coating chicken doesn't have to be time-consuming. This recipe adds lots of great flavor to budget-friendly chicken drumsticks by tossing them in a sealable bag with seasoning. With just a few minutes of prep and none of the mess, you'll enjoy crispy coated drumsticks cooked to perfection and a versatile meal that friends and family of all ages will love.

Hands-On Time: 5 minutes
Cook Time: 25 minutes

Serves 4

- ¾ cup all-purpose flour
- 2 cups plain panko
- 2 teaspoons light brown sugar, packed
- 1 teaspoon salt
- ½ teaspoon paprika
- ½ teaspoon garlic powder
- ¼ teaspoon onion powder
- ¼ teaspoon ground black pepper
- 1 tablespoon olive oil
- 8 chicken drumsticks

1. Preheat air fryer to 380°F.

2. Place all ingredients except olive oil and chicken in a large sealable bag. Close bag and shake to combine.

3. Brush each drumstick with olive oil. Working in batches, place 3–4 drumsticks in seasoning bag. Seal bag and shake to coat drumsticks as evenly as possible.

4. Place drumsticks in air fryer basket and cook 25 minutes, turning ⅔ of the way through cooking. When done, drumsticks will have an internal temperature of at least 165°F and will have a browned and crispy coating. Let rest 5 minutes, then serve warm.

PER SERVING

CALORIES: 512 | FAT: 19g | SODIUM: 524mg | CARBOHYDRATES: 30g | FIBER: 0g | SUGAR: 2g | PROTEIN: 48g

Chicken and Vegetable Casserole

Casseroles are a quick weeknight meal option, but the oven can really heat up the kitchen on hot days. Baking up your casserole in the air fryer will take less energy and still give you an amazing comfort-food meal in just 30 minutes.

Hands-On Time: 5 minutes
Cook Time: 20 minutes

Serves 4

- 2 cups cooked shredded chicken breast
- 2 cups frozen mixed vegetables
- ½ cup canned cream of chicken soup
- 2 tablespoons salted butter, melted
- ¾ cup water
- ½ teaspoon salt
- ½ teaspoon garlic powder
- ¼ teaspoon dried thyme
- ¼ teaspoon ground black pepper
- ¾ cup packaged French fried onions

1 Preheat air fryer to 350°F. Mix all ingredients except fried onions in a medium bowl until well combined.

2 Spray a 6" round baking pan with nonstick cooking spray and scrape chicken mixture into pan. Place pan in air fryer basket and cook 10 minutes.

3 Sprinkle fried onions on top and cook 10 more minutes. When done, mixture will be warm and bubbling. Let cool 5 minutes and serve.

PER SERVING

CALORIES: 312 | FAT: 15g | SODIUM: 700mg | CARBOHYDRATES: 15g | FIBER: 4g | SUGAR: 0g | PROTEIN: 25g

Cheesy Chicken Sliders

Ground chicken is an excellent alternative to beef and can often be found right next to the traditional cuts of chicken at the grocery store. This recipe is perfect for all flavor preferences, and you can easily switch gears to make these sliders into taco burgers by adding half a packet of taco seasoning. Or, for a different zesty twist, use an entire packet of ranch seasoning powder.

Hands-On Time: 5 minutes
Cook Time: 10 minutes

Yields 8

1½ pounds ground chicken breast
¼ cup grated Parmesan cheese
2 tablespoons mayonnaise
1 teaspoon salt
1 teaspoon chili powder
½ teaspoon dried oregano
¼ teaspoon ground black pepper
8 white slider buns
4 (1-ounce) slices mild Cheddar cheese, cut in half
8 leaves Bibb lettuce
2 medium beefsteak tomatoes, cut into ¼"-thick slices

1 Preheat air fryer to 380°F.

2 In a large bowl, mix chicken breast, Parmesan, mayonnaise, salt, chili powder, oregano, and pepper until well combined. Divide mixture into 8 equal portions and shape into patties 3" in diameter.

3 Working in batches as needed, place sliders in air fryer basket in a single layer and cook 10 minutes, turning halfway through cooking time. When done, internal temperature will be at least 165°F.

4 Place 1 slider onto each bun and top with cheese, lettuce, and tomatoes. Close buns and serve.

PER SERVING (SERVING SIZE: 1 SLIDER)

CALORIES: 317 | FAT: 16g | SODIUM: 607mg | CARBOHYDRATES: 20g | FIBER: 2g | SUGAR: 4g | PROTEIN: 24g

6

Beef and Pork Main Dishes

Beef and pork each star in so many dishes. They're easy to flavor, incredibly versatile, and totally delicious. Still, everyone's menu rotation can get a little stale after a while, and boring beef and pork dishes can leave a bad taste in the mouth. The good news, however, is that your air fryer is the perfect tool to help refresh your meals and breathe new life into your menu. This chapter does just that with wonderfully savory meals that are incredibly easy to make. From Coffee-Rubbed Steak to Pork Schnitzel, there's no shortage of amazing beef and pork options to spice up your meal plans.

French Bread Pepperoni Pizza

While the oven makes delicious pizzas, the air fryer takes them to the limit with mouthwatering browned and gooey cheese and an irresistibly crispy crust—all in less time than you'd need to preheat the oven. This convenient meal comes together in just 15 minutes, perfect for a late-night snack or low-effort meal that leaves you satisfied. Feel free to add your own toppings, such as black olives, cooked sausage crumbles, or a sprinkle of Parmesan.

Hands-On Time: 5 minutes
Cook Time: 10 minutes

Serves 6

¾ cup pizza sauce
1 (16-ounce) premade loaf French bread, sliced open lengthwise and cut into 6 even pieces
2 cups shredded mozzarella cheese
24 slices pepperoni
2 teaspoons Italian seasoning

1 Preheat air fryer to 250°F.

2 Spoon pizza sauce onto bread and evenly sprinkle cheese on top of sauce, then top with pepperoni.

3 Place pizzas in air fryer, working in batches as necessary. Cook 3 minutes, until cheese is melted, then increase temperature to 350°F for an additional 7 minutes. When pizza is done, cheese will be melted and edges will be brown and crispy. Garnish the pizza with Italian seasoning and serve warm.

PER SERVING

CALORIES: 349 | FAT: 9g | SODIUM: 900mg | CARBOHYDRATES: 44g | FIBER: 2g | SUGAR: 5g | PROTEIN: 17g

TEMPERATURE CHANGES

Air fryer fans are often powerful and can blow pizza toppings around. Not only can this affect your pizza; it can also cause burning and create a hazard. To avoid that issue, this recipe starts cooking the pizza at a low temperature (and, therefore, a lower fan speed). As the cheese melts, it helps the pepperoni stay in place, and we can increase the temperature with less concern about toppings flying around the basket.

Steak Kebabs

This recipe offers perfectly cooked steak and vegetables without the hassle of the grill. The air fryer gives the peppers' edges a beautiful char that caramelizes and enhances their natural sweetness. Metal skewers are ideal because they often come with air fryer accessory sets and they don't require any special preparation. If you use wooden skewers, soak them in water for 30 minutes before using them to reduce the chance of charring.

Hands-On Time: 10 minutes
Cook Time: 12 minutes

Serves 4

- 1½ pounds sirloin steak, cut into 1" cubes
- 2 medium red bell peppers, seeded and cut into 1" chunks
- 6 ounces cremini mushrooms (also called baby bellas), halved
- 1 medium yellow onion, peeled and cut into 1" chunks
- ¼ cup olive oil
- 1 teaspoon salt
- ½ teaspoon garlic powder
- ½ teaspoon dried oregano
- ½ teaspoon ground black pepper

1 Preheat air fryer to 320°F. Alternate pieces of steak, bell pepper, mushroom, and onion on 12 skewers until ingredients are fully used.

2 Lightly brush kebabs with olive oil and sprinkle with salt, garlic powder, oregano, and pepper evenly on all sides. Working in batches as needed, place kebabs in air fryer basket. Cook 12 minutes, turning when 3 minutes of cooking time remain. When done, vegetables will be browned at edges and steak will have an internal temperature of at least 145°F. Let rest 3 minutes, then serve.

PER SERVING (SERVING SIZE: 3 KEBABS)

CALORIES: 509 | FAT: 31g | SODIUM: 660mg | CARBOHYDRATES: 9g | FIBER: 2g | SUGAR: 4g | PROTEIN: 39g

Quick Meatball Subs

This recipe is a simplified way to enjoy a time-honored comfort-food dish. Crisped on the edges and melted to perfection, this easy sandwich will leave you feeling satisfied. Store-bought meatballs are used to make this dish easy to prepare, but feel free to make your own if you prefer. Simply add 4 minutes to the cooking time if using fresh homemade meatballs.

Hands-On Time: 10 minutes
Cook Time: 12 minutes

Serves 4

12 (1-ounce) frozen, fully cooked Italian-style meatballs
1 cup marinara sauce
4 (6") hoagie rolls
4 (1-ounce) slices provolone
1 teaspoon Italian seasoning
¼ cup grated Parmesan cheese

1 Preheat air fryer to 375°F.

2 Place meatballs in air fryer and cook 8 minutes, until heated through. Larger meatballs may need an additional 1–2 minutes.

3 Spread 2 tablespoons marinara inside each hoagie roll. Place a slice of provolone in each roll, and top each with 4 meatballs. Spoon an additional 2 tablespoons sauce into each sandwich.

4 Sprinkle each sandwich with Italian seasoning. Place sandwiches, buns open, in air fryer basket. Working in batches as necessary, cook sandwiches 4 minutes, until cheese is melted and buns are toasted.

5 Sprinkle sandwiches with Parmesan before folding in half. Serve warm.

PER SERVING

CALORIES: 610 | FAT: 32g | SODIUM: 1,453mg | CARBOHYDRATES: 48g | FIBER: 5g | SUGAR: 10g | PROTEIN: 30g

Sweet Heat Pork Chops

Elevate your pork chops with this simple recipe that fuses the sweetness of brown sugar with the smoky, subtle heat of chipotles. A light glaze makes these pork chops irresistibly delicious.

Hands-On Time: 10 minutes
Cook Time: 12 minutes

Serves 4

- 1 tablespoon light brown sugar, packed
- 1 tablespoon paprika
- 1 teaspoon garlic powder
- 1 teaspoon salt
- ¼ teaspoon ground black pepper
- ¼ teaspoon onion powder
- ¼ teaspoon ground mustard
- ¼ teaspoon chipotle chili powder
- 4 (4-ounce) boneless pork chops
- 1 tablespoon olive oil

1. Preheat air fryer to 400°F. In a small bowl, mix brown sugar, paprika, garlic powder, salt, pepper, onion powder, ground mustard, and chili powder until well combined.

2. Lightly brush each pork chop with olive oil, then sprinkle with spice mixture on each side.

3. Place pork chops in air fryer basket and cook 12 minutes, flipping halfway through cooking. When done, internal temperature will be at least 145°F and chops will be firm to the touch. Let rest 3 minutes and serve warm.

PER SERVING

CALORIES: 201 | FAT: 8g | SODIUM: 872mg | CARBOHYDRATES: 5g | FIBER: 1g | SUGAR: 4g | PROTEIN: 27g

Roast Beef and Cheddar Party Sliders

The air fryer makes these sliders warm, gooey, and full of flavor in just 10 minutes. The result can be a savory and convenient option for dinner or a fun snack to serve at a small gathering. Feel free to mix up the meat and use turkey, ham, or a mixed batch. Brushing the buns with butter ensures these sliders come out moist and rich; everyone will surely come back for more.

Hands-On Time: 5 minutes
Cook Time: 10 minutes

Serves 8

8 sweet Hawaiian-style rolls
½ cup mayonnaise
3 tablespoons yellow mustard
1 teaspoon Worcestershire sauce
16 (⅛"-thick) slices roast beef
8 (1-ounce) slices sharp Cheddar cheese
⅓ cup unsalted butter, melted

1 Preheat air fryer to 350°F. Slice each roll open horizontally.

2 For sauce, in a small bowl, whisk together mayonnaise, mustard, and Worcestershire sauce.

3 For each sandwich, generously brush bottom half of roll with sauce. Then layer 2 slices of roast beef, a slice of cheese, and top of roll.

4 Place sliders in air fryer basket. Brush all tops and sides with melted butter. Cook 10 minutes, until rolls are golden and cheese is melted and bubbling. Serve warm.

PER SERVING

CALORIES: 418 | FAT: 29g | SODIUM: 418mg | CARBOHYDRATES: 17g | FIBER: 0g | SUGAR: 5g | PROTEIN: 18g

Pineapple Brown Sugar–Glazed Ham

In the air fryer, a simple ham becomes a warm, spiced glazed ham, leaving your oven free to keep other food warm. This dish's focus is the pairing of sweetness with ham's innate salty, savory flavor. It's an incredibly easy family dinner entrée for a holiday or any day.

Hands-On Time: 5 minutes
Cook Time: 25 minutes

Serves 12

- ¾ cup light brown sugar, packed
- 1 (20-ounce) can pineapple slices in juice, drained, juice reserved
- ¼ teaspoon ground cloves
- ½ cup water
- 1 (4-pound) fully cooked boneless ham
- 6 maraschino cherries

1 Preheat air fryer to 320°F. In a medium bowl, whisk together brown sugar, pineapple juice, and cloves until evenly mixed.

2 Prepare a 6" round baking pan with cooking spray. Pour water in bottom of pan and place ham in pan. Brush all sides of ham generously with brown sugar mixture. Score four parallel diagonal lines across ham, about ¼" deep, then four more lines to make a crisscross pattern.

3 Place 6 pineapple slices on top of ham, and place a cherry in center of each ring, Secure each cherry with a toothpick.

4 Cook ham 25 minutes, brushing top with more brown sugar mixture every 5 minutes to achieve a thick glaze. When done, ham will be heated through and edges browned and caramelized. Slice and serve warm.

PER SERVING

CALORIES: 240 | FAT: 4g | SODIUM: 1,661mg | CARBOHYDRATES: 20g | FIBER: 0g | SUGAR: 19g | PROTEIN: 29g

Coffee-Rubbed Steak

If you've never used instant coffee in a spice rub, you're in for a treat. Coffee's rich flavors infuse easily and impart a ton of flavor to any cut of meat. The dry rub creates an incredible crust that makes every bite of this tender steak a triumph of bold flavor.

Hands-On Time: 5 minutes
Cook Time: 15 minutes

Serves 4

3 tablespoons instant coffee

3 tablespoons light brown sugar, packed

½ tablespoon smoked paprika

1 teaspoon garlic powder

1 teaspoon salt

1 teaspoon ground black pepper

¼ teaspoon onion powder

4 (6-ounce) New York strip steaks

4 tablespoons salted butter

1   Preheat air fryer to 400°F. In a small bowl, mix coffee, brown sugar, paprika, garlic powder, salt, pepper, and onion powder until well combined.

2   Rub spice mixture on both sides of each steak until well coated. Place steaks in air fryer basket and cook 15 minutes, turning when 5 minutes of cooking time remain. When done, edges will be firm and internal temperature will be at least 145°F, or 155°F for well-done.

3   Place a tablespoon of butter on top of each steak while still hot. Allow steaks to rest 5 minutes before serving.

PER SERVING

CALORIES: 402 | FAT: 17g | SODIUM: 763mg | CARBOHYDRATES: 13g | FIBER: 1g | SUGAR: 10g | PROTEIN: 42g

Garlicky Beef and Broccoli

This simple weeknight entrée is always a crowd-pleaser. Perfect in a bowl or on top of steamed rice, it's a staple dish that has a great balance of protein and vegetables, making it so satisfying. Coating the beef with cornstarch not only helps it crisp while cooking but also thickens the sauce once it's added and ensures that sauce coats the steak for terrific seasoning throughout.

Hands-On Time: 5 minutes
Cook Time: 10 minutes

Serves 4

¼ cup soy sauce
3 tablespoons light brown sugar, packed
3 cloves garlic, peeled and finely minced
1 tablespoon grated fresh ginger
1 pound flank steak, thinly sliced
½ teaspoon salt
¼ teaspoon ground black pepper
¼ cup cornstarch
2 cups fresh broccoli florets

1 Preheat air fryer to 400°F. In a small bowl, whisk together soy sauce, brown sugar, garlic, and ginger, then set aside.

2 Place steak in a large sealable bag and sprinkle with salt, pepper, and cornstarch. Seal bag and shake to coat each piece of steak.

3 Use tongs to lift steak slices from bag and shake off excess cornstarch, then place them in a 6" round baking pan. Cook 5 minutes, then add broccoli to pan and pour soy sauce mixture over beef and broccoli. Continue cooking 5 minutes, until beef has an internal temperature of at least 145°F (155°F for well-done) and broccoli is tender. Let rest 3 minutes, then serve warm.

PER SERVING

CALORIES: 267 | FAT: 7g | SODIUM: 1,087mg | CARBOHYDRATES: 19g | FIBER: 1g | SUGAR: 11g | PROTEIN: 28g

Barbecue Cheddar and Bacon Burgers

Spice up burger night with these amazing patties. These patties are filled with cheese, bacon, and onions; in other words, they're a flavor bonanza. Try them with Seasoned Curly Fries (Chapter 4) for a restaurant-worthy plate.

Hands-On Time: 10 minutes
Cook Time: 15 minutes

Serves 4

- 1½ pounds ground sirloin
- ¼ cup packaged French fried onions, finely crushed
- ¼ cup cooked medium bacon pieces
- ½ cup grated sharp Cheddar cheese
- 1 teaspoon salt
- ½ teaspoon ground black pepper
- 4 brioche buns, toasted
- 4 (1-ounce) slices sharp Cheddar cheese
- ½ cup barbecue sauce

1 Preheat air fryer to 370°F.

2 In a large bowl, mix together all ingredients except buns, Cheddar slices, and barbecue sauce. Separate mixture into 4 even sections. Then separate each section into 2 even balls. Press each ball into a 4" round patty.

3 Place burgers in air fryer basket fitted with parchment paper and cook 15 minutes, turning halfway through cooking time. When done, burgers will have an internal temperature of at least 160°F.

4 Place each burger on a bun and top with Cheddar and barbecue sauce. Serve warm.

PER SERVING

CALORIES: 563 | FAT: 18g | SODIUM: 1,606mg | CARBOHYDRATES: 48g | FIBER: 1g | SUGAR: 19g | PROTEIN: 50g

Pork Schnitzel

This recipe brings a delicious crunch and a pop of citrus to your dinner plate. These coated pork chops don't require a lot of ingredients, and they even have a simplified breading process to save you time. The juicy pork chops stay tender inside and form a deep golden brown crust with a craveable crunch.

Hands-On Time: 10 minutes
Cook Time: 12 minutes

Serves 4

- ½ cup all-purpose flour
- ½ tablespoon seasoned salt
- 1 cup plain panko
- 1 large egg
- 4 (6-ounce) boneless pork chops, pounded to ¼" thickness
- ½ teaspoon salt
- ½ teaspoon ground black pepper
- 1 medium lemon, cut into wedges
- 2 tablespoons chopped fresh parsley

1. Preheat air fryer to 400°F. In a medium bowl, whisk together flour, seasoned salt, and panko. In a second medium bowl, whisk egg.

2. Dip a pork chop in egg, then press firmly into flour and panko mixture to coat. Repeat with remaining pork chops. Sprinkle salt and pepper evenly on both sides of pork chops.

3. Place pork chops in air fryer basket and spray lightly with cooking spray. Cook 12 minutes, turning halfway through cooking. When done, pork chops will be golden brown and have an internal temperature of at least 145°F.

4. Let rest 3 minutes, garnish with lemon wedges and parsley, and serve warm.

PER SERVING

CALORIES: 380 | **FAT:** 8g | **SODIUM:** 861mg | **CARBOHYDRATES:** 26g | **FIBER:** 0g | **SUGAR:** 1g | **PROTEIN:** 43g

Italian Sausage and Pepper Hoagies

Sandwiches are a great time-saver and provide a filling meal without a lot of prep. These sandwiches showcase juicy Italian sausage and highlight the flavors with a trio of bell peppers, each contributing its own unique taste. You'll want to use fresh and fluffy hoagie rolls to support these hefty sandwiches.

Hands-On Time: 5 minutes
Cook Time: 15 minutes

Serves 4

1 medium yellow onion, peeled and sliced into ¼"-thick slices
1 medium yellow pepper, seeded and cut into ¼"-thick slices
1 medium red bell pepper, seeded and cut into ¼"-thick slices
1 medium green bell pepper, seeded and cut into ¼"-thick slices
4 (3-ounce) raw mild Italian sausage links
4 hoagie rolls
¼ cup salted butter, melted

ADD SOME SPICE
Adding pickled jalapeño pepper slices to the pepper and onion mix is a great way to add some heat to this meal.

1 Preheat air fryer to 400°F. Place onion and peppers in a 6" round baking pan, then layer sausage links on top.

2 Place pan in air fryer basket and cook 12 minutes, until sausages are fully cooked, with an internal temperature of at least 160°F, and vegetables are tender. Remove pan from air fryer basket and set aside.

3 Brush the inside of each hoagie roll with butter and place in air fryer basket, open, buttered side facing up. Cook 3 minutes, until buns are lightly toasted.

4 Nestle a sausage in each hoagie and top generously with peppers and onions. Serve warm.

PER SERVING

CALORIES: 583 | FAT: 34g | SODIUM: 1,165mg | CARBOHYDRATES: 47g | FIBER: 4g | SUGAR: 7g | PROTEIN: 22g

Hot Italian Wraps

Skip the takeout and opt for a much better, homemade version of your favorite sandwich restaurant's Italian wrap. Stacked with all the right toppings, each wrap is a savory feast that will tackle your hunger and satisfy your cravings. Feel free to add lettuce and tomatoes after cooking for a fresh crunch.

Hands-On Time: 5 minutes
Cook Time: 8 minutes

Serves 4

- ¼ cup olive oil
- 3 tablespoons red wine vinegar
- ¼ teaspoon Dijon mustard
- ½ teaspoon dried oregano
- 4 (42g) flatbread wraps
- 4 ounces Genoa salami, thinly sliced
- 4 ounces deli-style pepperoni, thinly sliced
- 4 ounces Black Forest ham, thinly sliced
- 4 (1-ounce) slices provolone cheese
- ¼ cup chopped pickled banana peppers
- ¼ cup salted butter, melted

1 Preheat air fryer to 375°F. Whisk together olive oil, red wine vinegar, mustard, and oregano until well combined and set aside.

2 Place wraps on a clean work surface. Add to each a layer of each slice of meat, using 3 ounces total per wrap. Add 1 slice of provolone to each wrap, and distribute the banana peppers among the wraps. Drizzle with olive oil mixture, then roll each wrap and secure with two toothpicks. Brush lightly with melted butter.

3 Place wraps in air fryer basket and cook 8 minutes, until cheese is melted and flatbread is lightly toasted. Serve warm.

PER SERVING

CALORIES: 635 | FAT: 49g | SODIUM: 1,757mg | CARBOHYDRATES: 21g | FIBER: 12g | SUGAR: 1g | PROTEIN: 32g

Hawaiian Pizza

When you need a filling meal, air fryer pizza is always a great option. It's incredibly easy to customize, and you can even assemble several pizzas and freeze them for when the mood strikes. This recipe uses white pizza sauce, similar to Alfredo sauce, for an amazingly creamy, cheesy bite, but feel free to use a traditional tomato-based sauce instead.

Hands-On Time: 5 minutes
Cook Time: 10 minutes

Serves 4

- 1 cup white pizza sauce
- 4 (6") pita rounds
- 2 cups shredded mozzarella cheese
- ½ cup shredded mild Cheddar cheese
- 8 ounces Canadian bacon, chopped
- ½ cup drained canned pineapple tidbits

1. Preheat air fryer to 370°F.

2. Spread ¼ cup pizza sauce on each pita round. Sprinkle ½ cup mozzarella and 2 tablespoons Cheddar on each pizza, then top with Canadian bacon and pineapple.

3. Working in batches as needed, place pizzas in air fryer basket. Cook 10 minutes, until cheese is browned and bubbling. Serve warm.

PER SERVING

CALORIES: 432 | FAT: 20g | SODIUM: 1,176mg | CARBOHYDRATES: 29g | FIBER: 1g | SUGAR: 8g | PROTEIN: 30g

Zesty Taco Meatballs

Meatballs are often flavored with Italian-style seasoning, but they can also be delicious when infused with a Mexican-style flavor combination. Enjoy these savory meatballs alongside rice or with bread for a creative and delicious spin on the meatball sub.

Hands-On Time: 10 minutes
Cook Time: 10 minutes

Serves 4

- 1 pound 80% lean ground beef
- ½ medium yellow onion, peeled and finely chopped
- ½ medium green bell pepper, seeded and finely chopped
- ¾ cup shredded medium Cheddar cheese
- ½ cup plain bread crumbs
- 3 tablespoons ranch seasoning
- 3 tablespoons taco seasoning

1. Preheat air fryer to 350°F. Mix all ingredients in a large bowl until well combined.

2. Form meatballs using 2 tablespoons of mixture apiece. Spray meatballs lightly with cooking spray and place in air fryer basket. Cook 10 minutes, shaking basket twice during cooking. When done, meatballs will be browned and have an internal temperature of at least 160°F. Serve warm.

PER SERVING

CALORIES: 406 | FAT: 18g | SODIUM: 1,377mg | CARBOHYDRATES: 20g | FIBER: 2g | SUGAR: 3g | PROTEIN: 29g

Puff Pastry Sausage Rolls

These buttery sausage rolls make for an easy, family-friendly dinner reminiscent of beef Wellington. Fluffy golden puff pastry is wrapped around savory Italian sausage in this three-ingredient recipe for a quick dinner that's both satisfying and flavorful.

Hands-On Time: 10 minutes
Cook Time: 12 minutes

Serves 4

1 (13.2-ounce) package puff pastry, thawed
½ pound mild Italian sausage
1 large egg, whisked

1 Preheat air fryer to 370°F. Cut puff pastry into 4 even pieces and poke each piece in three places with a fork, piercing halfway through the dough. Divide sausage into 4 even sections, then roll each section into a 1" × 3" log.

2 Place a sausage log along the long edge of each piece of puff pastry. Roll pastry around meat and press firmly to seal edges. Brush rolls lightly with egg wash and use a sharp knife to score each roll twice.

3 Place rolls in air fryer basket and cook 12 minutes, turning halfway through cooking. When done, sausage will have an internal temperature of at least 160°F and puff pastry will be golden brown. Serve warm.

PER SERVING

CALORIES: 515 | FAT: 36g | SODIUM: 884mg | CARBOHYDRATES: 32g | FIBER: 0g | SUGAR: 1g | PROTEIN: 15g

Supreme Calzones

If you want to switch up your routine while still taking advantage of all the goodness that pizza has to offer, these calzones are for you. Using refrigerated pizza dough makes the process super simple, and you're free to load them up however you choose. The possibilities stretch as far as your imagination.

Hands-On Time: 10 minutes
Cook Time: 15 minutes

Serves 4

- 2 tablespoons all-purpose flour
- 2 (13.8-ounce) tubes refrigerated pizza dough
- 40 slices pepperoni
- ⅓ pound cooked pork sausage, drained
- ½ medium green bell pepper, seeded and chopped
- ½ medium yellow onion, peeled and chopped
- 1½ cups shredded mozzarella

1 Preheat air fryer to 350°F. On a lightly floured work surface, unroll pizza dough and cut each piece in half, for a total of 4 rectangular pieces.

2 For each calzone, leaving a 1" border at the edges, top one half of a dough rectangle with 10 slices pepperoni and ¼ of the sausage, bell pepper, onion, and mozzarella. Fold dough over to cover fillings, and press edges together. Use a sharp knife to cut three vent holes in top of dough.

3 Place calzones in air fryer basket and cook 15 minutes, turning when 5 minutes of cooking time remain. Calzones will be firm and golden brown all over when done. Let cool 5 minutes, then serve warm.

PER SERVING

CALORIES: 849 | FAT: 32g | SODIUM: 2,066mg | CARBOHYDRATES: 102g | FIBER: 4g | SUGAR: 14g | PROTEIN: 33g

Bone-In Pork Chops

Making the perfect weeknight meal has never been simpler than with these thick-cut pork chops. Their natural flavors shine through and are elevated by a sweet and smoky spice rub that complements rather than overpowers the meat. These chops are juicy inside, while the edges are slightly crisped for a medley of tasty notes and textures you'll love.

Hands-On Time: 5 minutes
Cook Time: 20 minutes

Serves 4

- 2 tablespoons light brown sugar, packed
- 1 teaspoon salt
- 1 teaspoon smoked paprika
- ½ teaspoon garlic powder
- ½ teaspoon ground black pepper
- 4 (1-pound) bone-in pork chops, about 1½" thick
- 2 tablespoons butter, cut into 4 slices

WHY CHOOSE BONE-IN?

Sometimes people worry that bone-in cuts of meat may be more difficult to cook, but they're actually just as simple as boneless cuts. Plus, bone-in cuts have more flavor, retain moisture better, and are often less expensive than their boneless counterparts, making them a great option for anyone on a budget.

1 Preheat air fryer to 370°F. In a small bowl, mix brown sugar, salt, paprika, garlic powder, and pepper.

2 Sprinkle spice mixture over pork chops and gently press into meat. Place pork chops in air fryer basket and cook 15 minutes, then turn and cook 5 minutes more. When done, internal temperature will be at least 145°F and pork chops will look browned at the edges. Place a slice of butter on top of each pork chop. Let rest 3 minutes, then serve warm.

PER SERVING

CALORIES: 502 | FAT: 18g | SODIUM: 750mg | CARBOHYDRATES: 8g | FIBER: 0g | SUGAR: 7g | PROTEIN: 55g

Open-Faced Meatball Sandwiches

This recipe calls for beef meatballs, but feel free to use any cooked meatball you like, including chicken or pork, packaged or homemade. Dress up these sandwiches with your favorite cheese, such as freshly grated Parmesan, or a sprinkle of dried parsley, or even sliced basil for a fresh punch of herb flavor.

Hands-On Time: 5 minutes
Cook Time: 15 minutes

Serves 4

16 (1-ounce) frozen, fully cooked Italian-style beef meatballs
2 cups marinara sauce
1 teaspoon Italian seasoning
2 cloves garlic, peeled and finely minced
4 tablespoons salted butter, softened
8 slices Texas toast–style bread

1 Preheat air fryer to 400°F. Place meatballs in a 6" round baking pan, pour in marinara sauce, and stir gently to coat.

2 Place baking pan in air fryer and cook 10 minutes, stirring halfway through cooking. When done, meatballs will be heated throughout. Carefully remove baking pan and set aside.

3 In a small bowl, mix Italian seasoning, garlic, and butter until well combined. Spread a thin layer of mixture on one side of each slice of bread. Place bread slices in air fryer and cook 5 minutes at 400°F. When done, bread will be browned and crispy around edges.

4 Place 2 sauce-covered meatballs on top of each slice of bread and top with spoonfuls of remaining sauce from baking pan. Serve warm.

PER SERVING

CALORIES: 721 | FAT: 37g | SODIUM: 1,820mg | CARBOHYDRATES: 62g | FIBER: 7g | SUGAR: 16g | PROTEIN: 26g

Peach-Glazed Ribs

Always a game-day favorite, these ribs advance to the championship bracket with a sweet addition: fruit preserves. Sweet peaches and spicy chipotle chili powder fill these juicy ribs with perfectly balanced flavor. Try apricot preserves if you like a more tart flavor profile.

Hands-On Time: 5 minutes
Cook Time: 25 minutes

Serves 4

- ½ cup peach preserves
- 2 tablespoons apple cider vinegar
- 2 tablespoons light brown sugar, packed
- 1 teaspoon chipotle chili powder
- 1 teaspoon salt
- ½ teaspoon garlic powder
- ½ teaspoon ground black pepper
- 1 (2-pound) rack pork ribs, white membrane removed, halved

1 Preheat air fryer to 400°F.

2 In a medium bowl, whisk together peach preserves, vinegar, brown sugar, chili powder, salt, garlic powder, and pepper. Generously brush both sides of ribs with mixture until well coated.

3 Place ribs in air fryer basket, working in batches as necessary. Cook 25 minutes, until internal temperature reaches at least 190°F and no pink remains. Allow ribs to rest 5 minutes before cutting and serving.

PER SERVING

CALORIES: 582 | FAT: 34g | SODIUM: 684mg | CARBOHYDRATES: 33g | FIBER: 0g | SUGAR: 24g | PROTEIN: 28g

INTERNAL TEMPERATURE

While most pork products require an internal temperature of just 145°F (plus a 3-minute rest) to be considered safely cooked, ribs require a higher internal temperature for the best taste. Pork ribs' many tough fibers begin to break down once they reach 190°F. For fall-off-the-bone ribs, cooking until the internal temperature is slightly over 200°F will allow the fat to fully render and connective tissues to soften.

Steak Fajitas

Fajitas are always a crowd-pleaser. Tender-crisp vegetables and moist strips of steak are a simple combination but pack a ton of flavor into warm flour tortillas. Lime juice adds a bright and fresh element to the dish and elevates the other ingredients, taking these fajitas over the top.

Hands-On Time: 10 minutes
Cook Time: 8 minutes

Serves 4

1 pound sirloin steak, cut into ¼"-thick slices
½ teaspoon salt
½ teaspoon ground black pepper
1 medium white onion, peeled and cut into ¼"-thick slices
1 medium green bell pepper, seeded and cut into ¼"-thick slices
1 medium red bell pepper, seeded and cut into ¼"-thick slices
1 (1-ounce) packet dry fajita seasoning
2 tablespoons olive oil
Juice of 1 medium lime
8 (6") flour tortillas, warmed

1 Preheat air fryer to 400°F. Place steak in a large bowl and sprinkle with salt and black pepper.

2 Add onion and bell peppers to bowl and toss to combine. Sprinkle with fajita seasoning and drizzle evenly with olive oil. Toss to coat meat and vegetables.

3 Spray air fryer basket with cooking spray and scrape meat and vegetables into air fryer basket. Cook 8 minutes, shaking basket twice during cooking. When done, steak will be browned and vegetables will be tender with a slight crunch.

4 Pour lime juice evenly over fajita filling. Add filling evenly to tortillas and serve warm.

PER SERVING

CALORIES: 521 | FAT: 22g | SODIUM: 1,210mg | CARBOHYDRATES: 42g | FIBER: 3g | SUGAR: 5g | PROTEIN: 30g

New York Strip Steak with Herb Butter

Steak is a versatile entrée option that can be enjoyed on a regular day or served as a treat on special occasions. It's a naturally flavorful cut of meat, so it doesn't need a lot of extra seasoning. Adding herbed butter, however, is a gourmet finishing touch, and it ensures that the steak stays moist and has a rich overall taste.

Hands-On Time: 5 minutes
Cook Time: 10 minutes

Serves 4

¼ cup salted butter, softened
1 tablespoon lemon zest
1 teaspoon Worcestershire sauce
1 teaspoon Italian seasoning
4 (6-ounce) New York strip steaks
1 tablespoon olive oil
1 teaspoon salt
½ teaspoon ground black pepper

1 Preheat air fryer to 400°F.

2 Add butter, lemon zest, Worcestershire sauce, and Italian seasoning to a small bowl and fold seasonings into butter until well combined, then set aside.

3 Drizzle steaks with olive oil and sprinkle with salt and pepper. Place steaks in air fryer basket and cook 10 minutes, turning halfway through cooking. When done, steaks will have an internal temperature of at least 145°F (155°F for well-done).

4 Place steaks on serving plates and top with herb butter. Allow to rest 5 minutes before slicing and serving.

PER SERVING

CALORIES: 380 | FAT: 21g | SODIUM: 772mg | CARBOHYDRATES: 1g | FIBER: 0g | SUGAR: 0g | PROTEIN: 41g

Mini Meatloaves

These mini versions of the beloved dish take less time to prepare. The air fryer beautifully caramelizes the tomato topping and cooks the meat to perfection, making even meatloaf skeptics new fans. These loaves are full of natural flavor that pairs with a world of side dishes, from mashed potatoes to mac and cheese. Just don't forget the Twenty-Minute Dinner Rolls (Chapter 4).

Hands-On Time: 10 minutes
Cook Time: 15 minutes

Serves 4

- 1 pound 80% lean ground beef
- ⅓ cup Italian-style bread crumbs
- 1 large egg
- ½ cup chopped yellow onion
- ¾ teaspoon salt
- ¼ teaspoon ground black pepper
- 2 teaspoons Italian seasoning
- ¼ cup tomato paste
- 2 tablespoons light brown sugar, packed
- 2 tablespoons barbecue sauce
- ½ teaspoon yellow mustard

1 Preheat air fryer to 370°F. In a large bowl, mix beef, bread crumbs, egg, onion, salt, pepper, and Italian seasoning until well combined. Separate mixture into 4 portions and form each into a loaf shape.

2 In a small bowl, whisk together tomato paste, brown sugar, barbecue sauce, and mustard until smooth. Brush generously onto top of each loaf. Place loaves in air fryer basket and cook 15 minutes, until internal temperature is at least 160°F and juices run clear. Serve warm.

PER SERVING

CALORIES: 334 | FAT: 13g | SODIUM: 886mg | CARBOHYDRATES: 22g | FIBER: 2g | SUGAR: 13g | PROTEIN: 25g

Fish and Seafood Main Dishes

Fish and seafood may seem difficult to master, but your air fryer makes it easier than ever to bring all the goodness of a seaside restaurant right to your own kitchen. Whether you're looking for quick and crispy entrées or a deeply flavorful feast, there's no shortage of amazing options that you can whip up whenever you have a hankering. No matter your skill level, your air fryer can help you create delicious, restaurant-quality dishes in no time. From Spicy Salmon Patties to Honey Lemon Pepper Shrimp, this chapter will fulfill all of your seafood cravings and have you swimming back for more!

Honey Lemon Pepper Shrimp

The sweet and sticky sauce infuses its flavor into the shrimp while letting the seafood's natural taste shine. Lemon pepper shrimp is a favorite of seafood lovers, and this recipe adds a sweet twist that makes it soar. For a spicy flair, try swapping with hot honey, which is infused with dried chili peppers and can be found at most grocery stores.

Hands-On Time: 5 minutes
Cook Time: 8 minutes

Serves 4

2 tablespoons honey
1 tablespoon soy sauce
1 tablespoon sriracha
2 cloves garlic, peeled and finely minced
½ teaspoon salt
½ teaspoon freshly cracked black pepper
1 tablespoon lemon zest
1 pound uncooked medium shrimp, shelled and deveined
¼ cup chopped green onions

1   Preheat air fryer to 400°F. In a large bowl, whisk together honey, soy sauce, sriracha, garlic, salt, pepper, and lemon zest until well combined.

2   Place shrimp in mixture and gently toss to coat. Place shrimp in air fryer basket in an even layer. Cook 8 minutes, turning ⅔ of the way through cooking time. When done, shrimp will be opaque pink and C-shaped, and internal temperature will be at least 145°F. Serve warm, garnished with green onions.

PER SERVING

CALORIES: 110 | FAT: 1g | SODIUM: 1,132mg | CARBOHYDRATES: 12g | FIBER: 0g | SUGAR: 10g | PROTEIN: 14g

RAW SHRIMP

This recipe calls for raw shrimp that have the shells and main brown veins removed. Don't use precooked shrimp for this recipe; raw shrimp will absorb flavor as they cook, but precooked shrimp won't. So make sure to find the uncooked variety, which appear gray, never pink.

Spicy Salmon Patties

This recipe uses sriracha, a hot chili sauce, *and* a fresh jalapeño to provide the spicy flavor. Serve with a mild rice or mashed potatoes to balance the spice.

Hands-On Time: 5 minutes
Cook Time: 10 minutes

Serves 4

- 12 ounces canned pink salmon, well drained
- ½ cup plain bread crumbs
- 1 large egg
- ¼ cup mayonnaise
- 2 cloves garlic, peeled and finely minced
- 2 tablespoons sriracha
- ½ small jalapeño, seeded and finely diced
- ½ teaspoon salt
- ¼ teaspoon ground black pepper

1 Preheat air fryer to 375°F. In a large bowl, flake salmon into small pieces. Mix in bread crumbs, egg, mayonnaise, garlic, sriracha, and jalapeño until well combined.

2 Separate mixture into 4 even portions and shape into 1"-thick patties. Sprinkle each patty with salt and pepper, then place in air fryer basket. Cook 10 minutes, turning halfway through cooking. When done, patties will be lightly browned and firm. Serve warm.

PER SERVING

CALORIES: 303 | FAT: 16g | SODIUM: 959mg | CARBOHYDRATES: 12g | FIBER: 1g | SUGAR: 3g | PROTEIN: 25g

Jumbo Shrimp

Jumbo shrimp cook only slightly longer than the average-sized shrimp, and using your air fryer is the best way to get a perfect dish in minutes.

Hands-On Time: 5 minutes
Cook Time: 10 minutes

Serves 4

- 1 pound uncooked jumbo shrimp, peeled and deveined
- ¼ cup lemon juice
- 2 tablespoons unsalted butter, melted
- 2 teaspoons Old Bay Seasoning
- 3 cloves garlic, peeled and finely minced
- 2 teaspoons dried parsley

1 Preheat air fryer to 370°F. Place shrimp in a 6" round baking pan and pour lemon juice and butter on top. Sprinkle with Old Bay, garlic, and parsley.

2 Place pan in air fryer basket and cook 10 minutes, turning shrimp halfway through cooking. When done, shrimp will be opaque pink and C-shaped. Serve warm.

PER SERVING

CALORIES: 126 | FAT: 6g | SODIUM: 827mg | CARBOHYDRATES: 3g | FIBER: 0g | SUGAR: 0g | PROTEIN: 13g

Cajun-Spiced Tilapia

Tilapia is a nutrient-rich fish that's high in vitamin B$_{12}$ and mild in flavor. Serve with Crispy Lemon Broccoli (Chapter 4) for a well-rounded meal.

Hands-On Time: 5 minutes
Cook Time: 10 minutes

Serves 4

1 teaspoon smoked paprika
1 teaspoon dried thyme
½ teaspoon garlic powder
½ teaspoon ground black pepper
½ teaspoon salt
¼ teaspoon onion powder
¼ teaspoon cayenne pepper
4 (6-ounce) tilapia fillets
2 tablespoons salted butter, melted

1 Preheat air fryer to 350°F. In a small bowl, whisk together paprika, thyme, garlic powder, pepper, salt, onion powder, and cayenne until well combined.

2 Brush each piece of tilapia with butter and sprinkle generously with spice mixture. Place in air fryer basket and cook 10 minutes. When done, fish will flake easily and have an internal temperature of at least 145°F. Serve warm.

PER SERVING

CALORIES: 218 | FAT: 8g | SODIUM: 424mg | CARBOHYDRATES: 1g | FIBER: 0g | SUGAR: 0g | PROTEIN: 34g

Lemon Butter Rainbow Trout

This simple lemon butter trout is a great way to change up your meal plan. If fresh trout isn't available in your area, feel free to use previously frozen trout that has been thawed, or substitute with salmon.

Hands-On Time: 5 minutes
Cook Time: 8 minutes

Serves 4

4 (4-ounce) skin-on rainbow trout fillets
2 tablespoons salted butter, melted
1 tablespoon Old Bay Seasoning
2 cloves garlic, peeled and finely minced
1 medium lemon, zested and cut into 8 slices

1 Preheat air fryer to 370°F.

2 With skin sides down, brush each fillet with butter, then sprinkle with Old Bay. Scatter garlic and lemon zest on top of fillets.

3 Place 2 lemon slices on each fillet and place in air fryer with skin sides down. Cook 8 minutes, until trout flakes easily and has an internal temperature of at least 145°F. Serve warm.

PER SERVING

CALORIES: 186 | FAT: 9g | SODIUM: 500mg | CARBOHYDRATES: 0g | FIBER: 0g | SUGAR: 0g | PROTEIN: 23g

Sweet and Spicy Gochujang Salmon Fillets

Gochujang is a Korean fermented red pepper paste that offers the perfect blend of sweet and spicy. Combining it with buttery smooth salmon creates a flavor explosion that you'll quickly come to crave.

Hands-On Time: 5 minutes
Cook Time: 12 minutes

Serves 4

2 tablespoons soy sauce
2 tablespoons gochujang
1 tablespoon olive oil
2 cloves garlic, peeled and finely minced
1 tablespoon honey
2 teaspoons grated fresh ginger
¼ teaspoon salt
4 (4-ounce) salmon fillets, skin removed
1 scallion, thinly sliced

1 Preheat air fryer to 350°F. In a small bowl, whisk together soy sauce, gochujang, olive oil, garlic, honey, and ginger to form a paste.

2 Sprinkle salt on salmon fillets, then brush all sides of each fillet generously with spice paste. Place salmon in air fryer basket and cook 8 minutes. Open air fryer, brush salmon with a second layer of paste, and cook an additional 4 minutes. When done, salmon will flake easily and have an internal temperature of at least 145°F. Garnish with sliced scallion. Serve warm.

PER SERVING

CALORIES: 229 | FAT: 10g | SODIUM: 672mg | CARBOHYDRATES: 7g | FIBER: 0g | SUGAR: 5g | PROTEIN: 24g

GOCHUJANG ALTERNATIVES

For a spicy alternative, you can easily swap in sriracha, harissa, or chili-garlic sauce. If you want to skip the spice altogether, you can simply omit it without making further changes.

Air-Fried Trout

Old Bay Seasoning is an easy shortcut that adds lots of flavor to this dish, making it an effortless meal option that doesn't sacrifice taste. This recipe calls for skinless trout fillets, but feel free to leave the skin on and remove after cooking to lock in even more flavor.

Hands-On Time: 5 minutes
Cook Time: 12 minutes

Serves 4

- 4 (4-ounce) trout fillets, skin removed
- 2 tablespoons olive oil
- 2 teaspoons Old Bay Seasoning
- ½ teaspoon salt
- ¼ teaspoon ground black pepper

1 Preheat air fryer to 370°F. Brush each trout fillet with olive oil. Sprinkle both sides of each fillet with Old Bay, salt, and pepper.

2 Place fillets in air fryer basket and cook 12 minutes, turning halfway through cooking. When done, internal temperature will be 145°F and fillets will flake easily. Serve warm.

PER SERVING

CALORIES: 227 | FAT: 13g | SODIUM: 629mg | CARBOHYDRATES: 0g | FIBER: 0g | SUGAR: 0g | PROTEIN: 24g

Cheesy Tuna Patties

As you dig into these patties, every element—juicy tuna, crispy panko, gooey cheese—will remind you of your favorite tuna melt. Serve with a side salad to add a bright freshness to your meal.

Hands-On Time: 5 minutes
Cook Time: 8 minutes

Serves 4

- 24 ounces canned tuna, well drained
- ¼ cup plain panko
- 1 large egg
- 1 tablespoon mayonnaise
- ½ cup shredded sharp Cheddar cheese
- ½ teaspoon salt
- ¼ teaspoon ground black pepper

1 Preheat air fryer to 370°F. In a large bowl, mix all ingredients until well combined. Separate mixture into 4 even portions, then shape into 4" patties.

2 Place patties in air fryer basket and cook 8 minutes, until lightly browned and firm to the touch. Serve warm.

PER SERVING

CALORIES: 215 | FAT: 8g | SODIUM: 731mg | CARBOHYDRATES: 5g | FIBER: 0g | SUGAR: 0g | PROTEIN: 29g

Cilantro Lime Salmon

The combination of cilantro and lime doubles down on zingy, citrusy flavor while also imparting subtle herbal notes. This combination is a bright and unique take on the traditional use of lemon and herbs. The edges of the tender salmon caramelize during cooking and stand out as a satisfying contrast to the flaky interior.

Hands-On Time: 5 minutes
Cook Time: 12 minutes

Serves 4

1 (1-pound) salmon fillet, skin on
2 tablespoons olive oil
1 medium lime, halved
Zest of 1 medium lime
1 teaspoon ground paprika
1 teaspoon chili powder
½ teaspoon salt
¼ teaspoon ground black pepper
2 tablespoons chopped fresh cilantro

1   Preheat air fryer to 350°F. Place salmon fillet skin-side down on a piece of aluminum foil cut to fit air fryer. Brush fillet with olive oil, and squeeze juice of half of lime over salmon.

2   Sprinkle salmon evenly with lime zest, paprika, chili powder, salt, and pepper, and gently rub into fillet. Place salmon with foil in air fryer basket and cook 12 minutes, until salmon flakes easily and has an internal temperature of at least 145°F.

3   Garnish with remaining lime half, sliced into wedges, and chopped cilantro. Serve warm.

PER SERVING

CALORIES: 225 | FAT: 13g | SODIUM: 359mg | CARBOHYDRATES: 1g | FIBER: 1g | SUGAR: 0g | PROTEIN: 23g

Citrus-Glazed Sea Bass

Orange's natural sweetness and sea bass's richness combine to make this easy-to-prep dish. Sea bass absorbs flavors well, so you can enjoy a citrus zing through and through.

Hands-On Time: 5 minutes
Cook Time: 10 minutes

Serves 4

- ½ cup pulp-free orange juice
- 2 tablespoons soy sauce
- 2 cloves garlic, peeled and finely minced
- 3 tablespoons salted butter, melted
- 4 (6-ounce) sea bass fillets, skin removed
- ½ teaspoon salt
- ½ teaspoon paprika
- ¼ teaspoon ground black pepper
- 1 medium orange, cut into ¼"-thick slices

1 Preheat air fryer to 350°F. In a small bowl, whisk together orange juice, soy sauce, garlic, and butter until well combined and set aside.

2 Place sea bass in a 6" baking pan and sprinkle with salt, paprika, and pepper. Pour orange juice mixture over fillets and top each with a slice of orange.

3 Place pan in air fryer basket and cook 10 minutes. Use a silicone pastry brush to brush pan liquid over sea bass twice during cooking. When done, internal temperature will be at least 145°F and fish will flake easily with a fork. Serve warm.

PER SERVING

CALORIES: 191 | FAT: 4g | SODIUM: 456mg | CARBOHYDRATES: 5g | FIBER: 1g | SUGAR: 4g | PROTEIN: 32g

Sweet Chili Shrimp and Vegetables

This dish is great for those who enjoy stir-fry but want a more hands-off approach. The vegetables remain tender-crisp, making for an excellent texture contrast with the juicy shrimp. Feel free to add your favorite vegetables and enjoy this dish alone or on top of steamed rice.

Hands-On Time: 5 minutes

Cook Time: 4 minutes

Serves 4

- 1 medium zucchini, chopped
- 1 medium red bell pepper, seeded and chopped into ½" pieces
- ½ medium onion, peeled and cut into ½" pieces
- 1 pound uncooked medium shrimp, peeled and deveined
- ⅓ cup Thai sweet chili sauce
- ½ teaspoon salt
- ¼ teaspoon ground ginger

1 Preheat air fryer to 400°F.

2 Place all ingredients in 6" round baking pan and stir to combine. Place pan in air fryer basket and cook 4 minutes, until shrimp become C-shaped and bright pink. When done, vegetables will be tender-crisp. Serve warm.

PER SERVING

CALORIES: 144 | FAT: 1g | SODIUM: 1,167mg | CARBOHYDRATES: 18g | FIBER: 1g | SUGAR: 15g | PROTEIN: 14g

Crab Cakes

Crispy on the outside and abundant with soft bits of crab, this dish mixes up quickly and cooks in just 10 minutes. Crab has a delicate taste that's easily overwhelmed, so these cakes use just a few ingredients to bind the crab meat and boost its natural brininess. Be sure to look for lump crab meat—it has thicker pieces of crab that stay moist, are more flavorful, and contain less fillers than packages only labeled as "crab."

Hands-On Time: 5 minutes
Cook Time: 10 minutes

Serves 4

- 16 ounces lump crab meat, well drained
- ½ cup plain panko
- ¼ cup mayonnaise
- ¼ cup chopped red bell pepper
- 2 tablespoons lemon juice
- 2 teaspoons Old Bay Seasoning
- ½ teaspoon Dijon mustard

1 Preheat air fryer to 380°F. Mix all ingredients in a large bowl until well combined.

2 Separate mixture into 4 even sections and shape into ½"-thick patties, each about 5" wide.

3 Spray air fryer basket with nonstick cooking spray and place crab cakes in basket. Cook 10 minutes, turning halfway through cooking. When done, crab cakes will be lightly browned and firm. Serve warm.

PER SERVING

CALORIES: 230 | **FAT:** 11g | **SODIUM:** 969mg | **CARBOHYDRATES:** 11g | **FIBER:** 0g | **SUGAR:** 1g | **PROTEIN:** 20g

Salmon Tacos

Salmon is rich in omega-3s, making your next taco night not only delicious but nutritious too. Zingy lime juice elevates the buttery flavor of the salmon for a light and fresh-tasting meal. Crunchy slaw tops these tacos and adds a vibrant garnish that complements the tender salmon perfectly.

Hands-On Time: 5 minutes
Cook Time: 10 minutes

Serves 4

- 4 (4-ounce) salmon fillets, skin removed
- 1 tablespoon olive oil
- 1 teaspoon chili powder
- ½ teaspoon cumin
- ½ teaspoon salt
- ¼ teaspoon ground black pepper
- 2 cups pre-chopped, bagged coleslaw mix
- ¼ cup mayonnaise
- 2 tablespoons chopped fresh cilantro
- 2 tablespoons lime juice
- 12 white corn tortillas, warmed

1 Preheat air fryer to 375°F. Rub each side of salmon with olive oil and sprinkle with chili powder, cumin, salt, and pepper.

2 Place salmon in air fryer basket and cook 10 minutes, turning halfway through cooking. When done, salmon will have an internal temperature of at least 145°F and flake easily.

3 In a small bowl, mix coleslaw mix, mayonnaise, cilantro, and lime juice until well combined. Break salmon into bite-sized pieces and place on tortillas. Top with slaw and serve warm.

PER SERVING

CALORIES: 458 | FAT: 22g | SODIUM: 489mg | CARBOHYDRATES: 36g | FIBER: 6g | SUGAR: 2g | PROTEIN: 27g

Sesame-Crusted Tuna Steak

These tuna steaks are an incredibly simple but impressive option when it comes to dinner. The crispy sesame seed exterior locks in moisture and adds a great crunch while also giving the dish a restaurant-worthy presentation. Be sure to look for sashimi-grade tuna steak, especially if you plan to cook the fish to medium rather than well-done.

Hands-On Time: 5 minutes
Cook Time: 10 minutes

Serves 4

- 2 tablespoons olive oil
- 2 tablespoons soy sauce
- ½ teaspoon salt
- ⅓ cup white sesame seeds
- 3 tablespoons black sesame seeds
- 4 (6-ounce) yellowfin tuna steaks

HOW TO SERVE

Tuna steaks taste delicious by themselves, but dipping sauce can upgrade their flavor. Choose a sauce that complements your side dish as well as the tuna. Salty-savory soy sauce, smoky-sweet ponzu, and spicy wasabi can all contribute to a flavorful dipping sauce. Ramp up the presentation even more with a side of pickled ginger.

1 Preheat air fryer to 400°F. In a medium bowl, whisk together olive oil and soy sauce and set aside. Mix salt and both types of sesame seeds in a shallow medium bowl.

2 Pat each tuna steak dry with a paper towel. Dip each tuna steak in olive oil mixture, then press firmly in sesame seed mixture to coat.

3 Working in batches as needed, place tuna steaks in air fryer basket. Cook 10 minutes for well-done tuna steaks. When done, internal temperature will be at least 145°F and tuna steak will be pale pink. Serve warm.

PER SERVING

CALORIES: 356 | **FAT:** 16g | **SODIUM:** 808mg | **CARBOHYDRATES:** 5g | **FIBER:** 2g | **SUGAR:** 0g | **PROTEIN:** 45g

Dijon and Herb Lobster Tails

Lobster tails aren't just restaurant food; they're super simple to make at home with a few easy steps. These lobster tails remain juicy and full of succulent buttery flavor. Dijon mustard livens up the lobster meat with a hint of tang that balances the dish's richness. Make it a surf-and-turf night by air frying New York strip steaks to eat alongside the lobster tails.

Hands-On Time: 5 minutes
Cook Time: 7 minutes

Serves 4

- 2 tablespoons salted butter, softened
- 1 tablespoon finely minced garlic
- 1 tablespoon finely chopped fresh dill
- 1 teaspoon Dijon mustard
- ¼ teaspoon salt
- ¼ teaspoon ground black pepper
- 2 tablespoons lemon juice
- 4 (6-ounce) lobster tails

CUT WITH CAUTION

Lobster tails can have sharp edges that easily cut your fingers. Cracking open the shells safely gets easier with practice—just be sure to use caution and pay attention to stray sharp pieces.

1 Preheat air fryer to 400°F.

2 In a small bowl, mix butter, garlic, dill, Dijon, salt, pepper, and lemon juice.

3 Carefully cut open lobster tails with kitchen scissors and pull back shells a little to expose meat. Brush butter mixture on each tail.

4 Place tails in air fryer basket and cook 7 minutes, until lobster is firm and opaque and internal temperature reaches at least 145°F. Serve warm.

PER SERVING

CALORIES: 145 | FAT: 6g | SODIUM: 701mg | CARBOHYDRATES: 1g | FIBER: 0g | SUGAR: 0g | PROTEIN: 19g

Blackened Cod

Typically cod is associated with delicate and light flavors, but it can be the perfect canvas for stronger notes as well.

Hands-On Time: 5 minutes
Cook Time: 10 minutes

Serves 4

1 tablespoon smoked paprika
1 teaspoon garlic powder
½ teaspoon onion powder
½ teaspoon salt
¼ teaspoon ground black pepper
¼ teaspoon dried thyme
⅛ teaspoon cayenne pepper
2 tablespoons olive oil
4 (6-ounce) cod fillets

1 Preheat air fryer to 400°F. In a small bowl, mix paprika, garlic powder, onion powder, salt, black pepper, thyme, and cayenne until well combined.

2 Brush olive oil all over each piece of cod and sprinkle spice seasoning generously on each side. Place fillets in air fryer basket. Cook 10 minutes, carefully turning halfway through cooking. When done, cod will flake easily and have an internal temperature of at least 145°F. Serve warm.

PER SERVING

CALORIES: 207 | FAT: 8g | SODIUM: 383mg | CARBOHYDRATES: 2g | FIBER: 1g | SUGAR: 0g | PROTEIN: 31g

Breaded Catfish Bites

These nuggets are firm and flaky inside, with a delightfully crisp exterior. Spice them up by adding ½ teaspoon of your favorite seasoning to the cornmeal mixture, and serve them with a generous side of chilled tartar sauce.

Hands-On Time: 5 minutes
Cook Time: 10 minutes

Serves 4

1 teaspoon smoked paprika
Zest of 1 lemon
½ teaspoon salt
¼ teaspoon ground black pepper
½ cup yellow cornmeal
¼ cup all-purpose flour
1 pound catfish fillets, cut into 1" cubes

1 Preheat air fryer to 370°F. Place all ingredients except catfish in a 1-gallon sealable bag. Shake to combine. Add catfish to bag and shake to evenly coat.

2 Spray catfish lightly with cooking spray and place in air fryer basket. Cook 10 minutes, turning halfway through cooking. When done, catfish will be golden brown and have an internal temperature of at least 145°F. Serve warm.

PER SERVING

CALORIES: 178 | FAT: 6g | SODIUM: 404mg | CARBOHYDRATES: 9g | FIBER: 1g | SUGAR: 0g | PROTEIN: 18g

Crispy Crab Rangoon

Often considered a Chinese takeout staple, crab Rangoon is a creamy delight for even the hesitant seafood eater. You might be surprised to know that imitation crab is typically used in this dish. It's budget-friendly, and its sweetness gives crab Rangoon its distinct taste. Ultra-crispy, browned wonton wrappers and creamy filling make these bites irresistible.

Hands-On Time: 10 minutes
Cook Time: 8 minutes

Serves 4

1 cup finely chopped imitation crab meat
4 ounces cream cheese, softened
½ teaspoon garlic powder
¼ teaspoon salt
16 (3" × 3") wonton wrappers
¼ cup water
3 tablespoons vegetable oil

1 Preheat air fryer to 400°F. In a small bowl, combine crab, cream cheese, garlic powder, and salt until well combined.

2 Place wonton wrappers on a clean work surface and place about 2 tablespoons of crab mixture in the center of each wonton wrapper. Use a pastry brush to wet edges of each wonton wrapper with water. Fold wrappers diagonally to form triangles, and press edges tightly to seal.

3 Lightly brush each wonton wrapper with oil and place in air fryer basket, working in batches as needed. Cook 8 minutes, turning halfway through cooking. When done, wrappers will be golden brown and crispy. Allow to cool 5 minutes before serving.

PER SERVING

CALORIES: 323 | FAT: 19g | SODIUM: 626mg | CARBOHYDRATES: 26g | FIBER: 1g | SUGAR: 3g | PROTEIN: 8g

Roasted Tomato Cod

This combination is perfect for busy meal times. Roasting cherry tomatoes enhances their sweetness, and they play the perfect counterpart to the mild and buttery cod. Fresh cod works best for this, but frozen is also an option—just be sure to defrost it in a bowl of cool water for 10 minutes before following the recipe steps.

Hands-On Time: 5 minutes
Cook Time: 10 minutes

Serves 4

4 (6-ounce) cod fillets
2 tablespoons olive oil
1 teaspoon dried oregano
½ teaspoon salt
1 cup cherry tomatoes
2 leaves fresh basil, thinly sliced

1 Preheat air fryer to 400°F. Spray a 6" round baking pan with nonstick cooking spray.

2 Brush cod fillets with olive oil and sprinkle with oregano and salt. Place fillets in pan and nestle cherry tomatoes among fillets. Place pan in air fryer basket and cook 10 minutes, carefully turning halfway through cooking. When done, cod will flake easily and have an internal temperature of 145°F and tomatoes will be soft and slightly burst open.

3 Top with basil and serve warm.

PER SERVING

CALORIES: 209 | **FAT:** 7g | **SODIUM:** 384 | **CARBOHYDRATES:** 2g | **FIBER:** 1g | **SUGAR:** 1g | **PROTEIN:** 31g

Crab-Stuffed Mushrooms

This delicious dish is an excellent appetizer but can also make a fun and flavorful entrée. Chunks of lump crab are stuffed into savory mushroom caps for a umami-packed dish. The creamy filling uses simple, easy-to-find ingredients that you likely already have in your pantry, making for a great last-minute meal.

Hands-On Time: 10 minutes
Cook Time: 10 minutes

Serves 4

- **16 cremini mushrooms (also called baby bellas), stems removed**
- **2 tablespoons olive oil**
- **1 (6-ounce) can lump crab meat, well drained**
- **½ cup plain panko**
- **2 ounces cream cheese, softened**
- **1 teaspoon Old Bay Seasoning**
- **½ teaspoon salt**
- **¼ teaspoon ground black pepper**
- **2 tablespoons chopped parsley**

1 Preheat air fryer to 350°F. Brush each mushroom cap all over with olive oil and set aside.

2 In a medium bowl, mix crab, panko, cream cheese, Old Bay, salt, and pepper until well combined. Place 1 tablespoon of mixture in each mushroom cap.

3 Place mushrooms in air fryer basket and cook 10 minutes. When done, mushrooms will be tender and mixture will be bubbling and browned. Garnish with parsley and serve.

PER SERVING

CALORIES: 200 | FAT: 11g | SODIUM: 684mg | CARBOHYDRATES: 14g | FIBER: 1g | SUGAR: 2g | PROTEIN: 10g

Bacon-Wrapped Shrimp

These juicy, flavor-packed shrimp are perfectly complemented by the smoky bacon they're wrapped in. Not only does this add up to an irresistible flavor combination, but the bacon's crisp texture makes for a pleasant crunch.

Hands-On Time: 10 minutes
Cook Time: 10 minutes

Serves 4

2 tablespoons light brown sugar, packed
1 teaspoon smoked paprika
½ teaspoon Old Bay Seasoning
¼ teaspoon onion powder
16 uncooked jumbo shrimp, peeled and deveined
8 slices bacon, halved crosswise

1 Preheat air fryer to 370°F. In a small bowl, mix brown sugar, paprika, Old Bay, and onion powder. Place shrimp in a medium bowl and sprinkle with seasoning mixture. Toss to coat evenly.

2 Wrap each shrimp with ½ slice bacon, securing with toothpicks. Place shrimp in air fryer basket, working in batches as needed. Cook 10 minutes, turning halfway through cooking. When done, bacon will be crispy, and shrimp will be opaque and C-shaped. Serve warm.

PER SERVING

CALORIES: 157 | FAT: 6g | SODIUM: 736mg | CARBOHYDRATES: 8g | FIBER: 0g | SUGAR: 7g | PROTEIN: 15g

Panko-Crusted Mahi Mahi

Punched up with citrus juice and subtle peppery seasoning, this crispy entrée can easily become a staple in your weeknight dinner rotation.

Hands-On Time: 5 minutes
Cook Time: 12 minutes

Serves 4

1 cup plain panko
2 teaspoons lemon pepper seasoning
½ teaspoon salt
4 (6-ounce) mahi mahi fillets, skin removed
2 tablespoons olive oil
1 medium lemon, cut into wedges

1 Preheat air fryer to 370°F. In a large shallow dish combine panko, lemon pepper seasoning, and salt.

2 Brush each fillet with olive oil and firmly press each side into panko mixture to coat. Place fillets in air fryer basket and cook 12 minutes. When done, fillets will be opaque, flake easily, and have an internal temperature of at least 145°F. Serve warm with lemon wedges on the side.

PER SERVING

CALORIES: 260 | FAT: 9g | SODIUM: 353mg | CARBOHYDRATES: 10g | FIBER: 0g | SUGAR: 1g | PROTEIN: 33g

8

Vegetarian Main Dishes

Whether you're simply looking to cut down on meat consumption or you're interested in a completely vegetarian meal, this chapter will help you craft easy, delicious, meat-free dishes. These aren't your run-of-the-mill vegetarian dishes; they're nutrient rich, incredibly flavorful, and completely satisfying, even if you're a meat eater. Best of all, thanks to your air fryer, all of the recipes in this chapter come with simple ingredients and just a few straightforward instructions so you can serve up a variety of meatless favorites in minutes! From Black Bean Taquitos to Feta Herb–Stuffed Tomatoes, this chapter will leave you in a state of meatless bliss.

Black Bean Taquitos

Many Mexican-style dishes include meat to give the meal more flavor and substance. In the case of these taquitos, however, the filling is so hearty and delicious, you won't even notice it's a meatless recipe! Serve with one or several excellent dipping options, such as queso, sour cream, or guacamole.

Hands-On Time: 10 minutes
Cook Time: 8 minutes

Serves 4

2 (15-ounce) cans black beans, drained and rinsed
½ cup shredded mild Cheddar cheese
¼ cup mild salsa
2 tablespoons premade taco seasoning
2 tablespoons lime juice
12 (4") yellow corn tortillas, warmed

HOW TO WARM TORTILLAS FOR ROLLING

Corn tortillas tend to break into pieces if you try to roll them when they're cold. To warm them sufficiently, simply place a stack of them on a plate, cover with a damp paper towel, and microwave for 60 seconds. They will be very warm but should bend and roll with ease without crumbling. If you find they do fall apart, place them back in the microwave for 20 more seconds.

1 Preheat air fryer to 350°F. In a large bowl, mash black beans until mostly smooth. Use a rubber spatula to fold in Cheddar, salsa, taco seasoning, and lime juice.

2 Place 3 tablespoons of mixture in a line near one end of each tortilla. Gently roll each tortilla up and place seam-side down in air fryer basket, securing with toothpicks if necessary. Lightly spray taquitos with cooking spray and cook 8 minutes, until golden brown and crispy. Serve warm.

PER SERVING

CALORIES: 365 | FAT: 5g | SODIUM: 750mg | CARBOHYDRATES: 59g | FIBER: 13g | SUGAR: 4g | PROTEIN: 18g

Eggplant Parmesan

If you've only experienced this dish's meat-based descendants, you're in for a treat. Hailing from early-1800s Naples, eggplant Parmesan layers traditional Italian flavors with mild, creamy, nutrient-rich eggplant. Enjoy this dish on its own, or serve it with pasta for a heartier meal.

Hands-On Time: 10 minutes
Cook Time: 20 minutes

Serves 4

2 large eggs
¾ cup grated Parmesan cheese, divided
1 cup Italian-style bread crumbs
1 large eggplant, sliced into ½"-thick rounds
1 teaspoon Italian seasoning
½ teaspoon garlic powder
½ teaspoon salt
1 cup marinara sauce
1 cup shredded mozzarella cheese
3 medium basil leaves, thinly sliced

1 Preheat air fryer to 370°F. Whisk eggs in a medium, shallow bowl. Place ½ cup Parmesan and bread crumbs in another medium shallow bowl.

2 Dip an eggplant slice in egg and allow excess to drip off. Press firmly into bread crumb mixture to completely coat on each side. Repeat with remaining eggplant slices.

3 Sprinkle both sides of eggplant slices with Italian seasoning, garlic powder, and salt. Spray lightly with cooking spray and place in air fryer basket. Cook 15 minutes, until browned and crispy.

4 Spread a spoonful of marinara sauce over each slice, then top each with mozzarella. Air fry an additional 5 minutes, until cheese is melted and bubbling. Sprinkle remaining 1/4 cup Parmesan and basil on top. Serve warm.

PER SERVING

CALORIES: 298 | FAT: 10g | SODIUM: 1,268mg | CARBOHYDRATES: 32g | FIBER: 6g | SUGAR: 10g | PROTEIN: 17g

Tofu Fajitas

One of the best things about tofu is that it completely takes on the flavors of the foods it's being cooked with. In this case, that means a crisped and crumbly plant-based protein that has rich fajita flavor all the way through. Enjoy these fajitas in a tortilla, or turn them into an easy bowl meal.

Hands-On Time: 5 minutes
Cook Time: 15 minutes

Serves 4

12 ounces pressed extra-firm tofu, cut into 4"-long-by-¼"-thick slices

1 medium green bell pepper, seeded and cut into ¼"-thick slices

1 medium red bell pepper, seeded and cut into ¼"-thick slices

1 medium yellow onion, peeled and cut into ¼"-thick slices

2 tablespoons olive oil

¼ cup fajita seasoning

1 medium lime, juiced

8 (6") flour tortillas, warmed

½ cup guacamole

½ cup sour cream

1 Preheat air fryer to 400°F. Place tofu, bell peppers, and onion in a large sealable bag. Pour in olive oil, fajita seasoning, and lime juice. Close bag and shake to coat all ingredients well.

2 Empty bag into air fryer basket and cook 15 minutes, shaking three times during cooking. When done, vegetables will be tender and tofu crisped at edges.

3 Place tofu and vegetables in tortillas and top with guacamole and sour cream. Serve warm.

PER SERVING

CALORIES: 522 | FAT: 28g | SODIUM: 958mg | CARBOHYDRATES: 47g | FIBER: 6g | SUGAR: 6g | PROTEIN: 21g

PRESSED TOFU
Pressing tofu allows excess water to drain and gives the tofu a firmer texture. You can use a traditional tofu press for this or simply wrap the tofu in a clean dish towel or paper towel and press under a cutting board for a few minutes.

Garlic Bread Grilled Cheese Sandwiches

Boost your grilled cheese into the stratosphere with an ultra-creamy cheese mixture. The result is so full of buttery, garlicky flavor and gooey Cheddar, it's not your simple childhood sandwich, but it's still a great comfort food that goes deliciously with warm tomato soup. Feel free to add your favorite cheese to the mix for a personalized recipe.

Hands-On Time: 5 minutes
Cook Time: 7 minutes

Serves 2

- 2 tablespoons salted butter, melted
- 2 tablespoons mayonnaise
- 1 tablespoon grated Parmesan cheese
- 2 teaspoons garlic paste
- ½ teaspoon dried parsley
- 4 slices Texas toast–style bread
- 4 (1-ounce) slices sharp Cheddar cheese

1 Preheat air fryer to 370°F. In a small bowl, mix butter, mayonnaise, Parmesan, garlic paste, and parsley until well combined.

2 Spread ¼ of mixture on one side of each bread slice. Assemble sandwiches, buttered sides of bread facing out, using 2 slices Cheddar per sandwich. Place in air fryer basket. Cook 7 minutes, turning halfway through cooking. When done, bread will be golden brown and cheese will be melted. Serve warm.

PER SERVING

CALORIES: 616 | FAT: 40g | SODIUM: 1,078mg | CARBOHYDRATES: 35g | FIBER: 2g | SUGAR: 4g | PROTEIN: 21g

Southwest Black Bean Burgers

Black bean burgers can be a staple of a vegetarian meal plan. Not only do they taste delicious, but they are also rich in fiber and protein to keep you full. This Southwest spin on the classic burger incorporates corn and green chilies for a delicious texture and flavor. Enjoy these burgers alone or on your favorite burger buns.

Hands-On Time: 10 minutes
Cook Time: 10 minutes

Serves 4

- 2 (14.5-ounce) cans black beans, drained and rinsed
- ¼ cup drained canned corn kernels
- 4 ounces drained canned green chilies
- 2 scallions, chopped
- 1 large egg
- ½ cup plain bread crumbs
- ½ teaspoon salt
- ¼ teaspoon ground black pepper
- 1 tablespoon fajita seasoning

1 Preheat air fryer to 370°F. In a large bowl, use a fork to mash beans until mostly broken down. Mix in remaining ingredients until well combined.

2 Separate mixture into 4 equal portions, then shape each into a patty about ½" thick. Lightly spray both sides of each patty with cooking spray and place in air fryer basket. Cook 10 minutes, turning halfway through cooking. When done, burgers will be firm and hold together. Serve warm.

PER SERVING

CALORIES: 285 | FAT: 2g | SODIUM: 818mg | CARBOHYDRATES: 50g | FIBER: 10g | SUGAR: 4g | PROTEIN: 16g

Crispy Tofu Bites

Whether you're enjoying a grain bowl or a salad, adding these flavorful bites brings a punch of flavor to any dish. Feel free to let these marinate all day so all you need to do before dinner is toss them into the air fryer.

Hands-On Time: 15 minutes
Cook Time: 10 minutes

Serves 4

¼ cup soy sauce
2 tablespoons honey
1 tablespoon sriracha
½ teaspoon salt
½ teaspoon garlic powder
¼ teaspoon ground ginger
1 pound extra-firm tofu, cut into ½" cubes

1 In a large bowl, whisk soy sauce, honey, sriracha, salt, garlic powder, and ginger until well combined. Toss tofu in mixture and let it marinate for at least 10 minutes.

2 Preheat air fryer to 400°F. Place tofu in air fryer basket and cook 10 minutes, until browned at the edges and crispy. Let cool 5 minutes, then serve warm.

PER SERVING

CALORIES: 186 | FAT: 9g | SODIUM: 636mg | CARBOHYDRATES: 10g | FIBER: 3g | SUGAR: 5g | PROTEIN: 19g

Garlic Butter Portobellos

Portobellos are a versatile ingredient. Enjoy these tender mushrooms alongside your favorite side dishes, or load them up with ingredients for super savory bowl meals.

Hands-On Time: 5 minutes
Cook Time: 5 minutes

Serves 4

4 large portobello mushrooms, stems and gills removed
1 tablespoon olive oil
2 tablespoons salted butter, melted
4 cloves garlic, peeled and finely minced
½ teaspoon salt
¼ teaspoon ground black pepper
2 tablespoons chopped fresh parsley

1 Preheat air fryer to 370°F. Brush each mushroom all over with olive oil. Place mushrooms top-side up in air fryer basket.

2 Generously drizzle butter over each mushroom and sprinkle with minced garlic, salt, and pepper. Cook 5 minutes, until tender. Garnish with parsley and serve warm.

PER SERVING

CALORIES: 103 | FAT: 9g | SODIUM: 345mg | CARBOHYDRATES: 4g | FIBER: 1g | SUGAR: 2g | PROTEIN: 2g

Feta Herb–Stuffed Tomatoes

This unique recipe is the perfect way to use those large summer tomatoes. A quick herbed stuffing fills the tomatoes with lots of flavor while keeping things fresh and easy. Feta crumbles melt into the filling for a gooey bite with a bit of tang that pairs perfectly with the sweet roasted-tomato taste.

Hands-On Time: 5 minutes
Cook Time: 10 minutes

Serves 4

- 4 large beefsteak tomatoes
- 1 cup cubed day-old French bread
- 2 cloves garlic, peeled and finely minced
- 2 tablespoons fresh chopped basil
- ½ cup crumbled feta cheese
- 2 tablespoons olive oil
- ½ teaspoon salt
- ¼ teaspoon ground black pepper

1 Preheat air fryer to 350°F. Cut off tops of tomatoes. Scoop out juice and seeds and discard.

2 In a medium bowl, combine bread, garlic, basil, feta, olive oil, salt, and pepper. Fill each tomato to the top with herb and bread mixture.

3 Place tomatoes in air fryer basket and cook 10 minutes, until cheese is melted and tomatoes are soft. Serve warm.

PER SERVING

CALORIES: 178 | FAT: 11g | SODIUM: 546mg | CARBOHYDRATES: 15g | FIBER: 3g | SUGAR: 6g | PROTEIN: 6g

Jalapeño Popper Grilled Cheese Sandwiches

Grilled cheese sandwiches are a staple when it comes to easy meals. Kick your classic up a notch with this spicy spin. Pickled jalapeños add a zesty bite and really cut down on prep time compared to preparing traditional poppers. You'll love this ultra-cheesy sandwich filled with all the flavors of a popper but without the hassle.

Hands-On Time: 5 minutes
Cook Time: 8 minutes

Serves 4

- 4 tablespoons cream cheese, softened
- ¼ teaspoon garlic powder
- 1 cup shredded mild Cheddar cheese
- ¼ cup shredded pepper jack cheese
- 2 tablespoons mayonnaise
- 8 (½"-thick) slices ciabatta
- ½ cup drained pickled jalapeño slices

1 Preheat air fryer to 380°F. In a medium bowl, mix cream cheese, garlic powder, Cheddar, and pepper jack until well combined.

2 Spread a light layer of mayonnaise on one side of each ciabatta slice. Place 4 slices mayonnaise-side down on a work surface, and spread ¼ of cheese mixture on each. Place slices of jalapeño on top of cheese mixture. Top sandwiches with remaining bread slices, mayonnaise-side up.

3 Place sandwiches in air fryer basket. Cook 8 minutes, carefully turning after 4 minutes. When done, sandwiches will be golden brown and cheese inside will be melted. Serve warm.

PER SERVING

CALORIES: 457 | FAT: 21g | SODIUM: 895mg | CARBOHYDRATES: 45g | FIBER: 3g | SUGAR: 2g | PROTEIN: 17g

Crispy Pesto Gnocchi

This recipe showcases gnocchi's versatility by embracing the incredible crispy texture they can take on in the air fryer. These gnocchi are coated in pesto before browning, leading to a flavor-packed dish that celebrates contrasting textures.

Hands-On Time: 5 minutes
Cook Time: 15 minutes

Serves 4

1 teaspoon paprika
½ teaspoon garlic powder
¼ cup basil pesto
1 pound frozen potato gnocchi
2 tablespoons grated Parmesan cheese

1 Preheat air fryer to 400°F.

2 In a large bowl, mix paprika, garlic powder, and pesto until well combined. Toss gnocchi in mixture, then place in air fryer basket. Cook 15 minutes, shaking basket three times during cooking. When done, gnocchi will be crisp to the touch. Let cool 5 minutes, then garnish with Parmesan to serve.

PER SERVING

CALORIES: 243 | FAT: 6g | SODIUM: 468mg | CARBOHYDRATES: 40g | FIBER: 2g | SUGAR: 1g | PROTEIN: 6g

Easy Vegetarian Chili Cheese Fries

This game-day dish comes together in minutes. Use your favorite canned chili for this recipe or go all out with a homemade batch. Load the fries up with your favorite toppings, such as chopped onions or sliced jalapeños.

Hands-On Time: 5 minutes
Cook Time: 15 minutes

Serves 4

12 ounces frozen French fries
1 (15-ounce) can vegetarian chili with beans
1 cup shredded mild Cheddar cheese

1 Preheat air fryer to 400°F. Cut a piece of aluminum foil to fit air fryer basket and place on a work surface.

2 Place fries on foil and top evenly with small spoonfuls of chili. Sprinkle with cheese, then place in air fryer basket. Cook 15 minutes, until fries are crispy and chili is heated through. Serve warm.

PER SERVING

CALORIES: 360 | FAT: 11g | SODIUM: 851mg | CARBOHYDRATES: 35g | FIBER: 6g | SUGAR: 3g | PROTEIN: 14g

Spinach-Stuffed Mushrooms

These poppable mushrooms make a satisfying, easy dinner, and they're great for parties as well. They have an earthy mushroom flavor, along with creamy, garlicky cheese that makes them extra-dreamy. Spinach adds color and fiber to this rich and cheesy dish.

Hands-On Time: 10 minutes
Cook Time: 10 minutes

Yields 16

- 1 cup firmly packed fresh spinach, chopped
- 4 ounces cream cheese, softened
- 3 cloves garlic, peeled and finely minced
- ¼ cup grated Parmesan cheese
- ½ teaspoon salt
- ¼ teaspoon ground black pepper
- 16 cremini mushrooms (also called baby bellas), stems removed

1 Preheat air fryer to 375°F. In a large bowl, mix spinach, cream cheese, garlic, Parmesan, salt, and pepper.

2 Spoon 1 tablespoon of mixture into each mushroom cap. Place mushrooms in air fryer basket and cook 10 minutes, until mushrooms are tender and cream cheese mixture is bubbling. Serve warm.

PER SERVING (SERVING SIZE: 4 MUSHROOMS)

CALORIES: 162 | FAT: 10g | SODIUM: 518mg | CARBOHYDRATES: 11g | FIBER: 2g | SUGAR: 2g | PROTEIN: 7g

Stuffed Peppers with Plant-Based Beef Crumbles

This is a quick and easy meal with high-impact flavor. Precooked beef-style plant-based crumbles make this recipe a breeze and can please meat eaters and vegetarians alike. Mushrooms add a touch of umami to this vegetable-packed dish, and they perfectly complement the savory elements of the marinara sauce, tying it all together with each earthy bite. Serve with extra marinara sauce to spoon over peppers.

Hands-On Time: 10 minutes
Cook Time: 15 minutes

Serves 4

- ½ pound precooked defrosted beef-style plant-based crumbles
- ½ cup sliced button mushrooms, chopped
- ¼ cup diced yellow onion
- 2 cups marinara sauce
- ½ teaspoon salt
- 1 teaspoon Italian seasoning
- 4 medium green bell peppers, tops, ribs, and seeds removed

1 Preheat air fryer to 380°F. In a medium bowl, mix plant-based crumbles, mushrooms, onion, marinara sauce, salt, and Italian seasoning until well combined.

2 Distribute mixture evenly among bell peppers. Place stuffed peppers in air fryer basket and cook 15 minutes, until peppers are tender and sauce mixture is bubbling at edges. Serve warm.

PER SERVING

CALORIES: 175 | FAT: 4g | SODIUM: 1,089mg | CARBOHYDRATES: 21g | FIBER: 7g | SUGAR: 11g | PROTEIN: 13g

PLANT-BASED CRUMBLES
Plant-based crumbles are usually found in the freezer section at the grocery store. If you need a simple alternative, cooked lentils can provide protein, fiber, and a delicious texture that complements this dish.

Bean and Cheese Quesadillas

While salsa often serves as the dipping sauce for quesadillas, this simple recipe includes it on the inside to impart its tomato-based flavor and help keep the dish from drying out. If you're in need of a speedy lunch, these quesadillas will keep you full all afternoon with just 15 minutes of total time spent. Serve with additional salsa, guacamole, and sour cream.

Hands-On Time: 5 minutes
Cook Time: 10 minutes

Serves 4

2 cups refried pinto beans
4 (8") flour tortillas
1 cup chunky mild salsa
2 cups shredded Mexican-blend cheese

REFRIED BEAN ALTERNATIVES

Feel free to use your favorite type of beans for this quesadilla. Refried beans are a simple option, but mashed black beans or even lentils will taste great in this recipe.

1 Preheat air fryer to 350°F. Spread ¼ cup refried beans on half of each tortilla. Spread 2 tablespoons salsa on top of refried beans.

2 Sprinkle cheese on each tortilla on top of salsa and fold in half. Spray both sides of each quesadilla with cooking spray and place in air fryer basket. Cook 10 minutes, turning halfway through cooking. When done, cheese will be melted and tortilla lightly browned. Serve warm.

PER SERVING

CALORIES: 466 | FAT: 19g | SODIUM: 1,436mg | CARBOHYDRATES: 46g | FIBER: 8g | SUGAR: 7g | PROTEIN: 23g

Simple Falafel

Crispy, browned exteriors and soft flavorful insides make these falafel a no-brainer for your weeknight meal plan. Falafel can be eaten in so many ways: dipped into tahini or yogurt-based sauce, stuffed into a vegetable-filled pita, or used as a delicious and textured addition to a green salad. This recipe simplifies the ingredients and process to make falafel prep easier than ever. Zhuzh them up, if you like, by adding a handful of fresh herbs such as parsley or dill and a sprinkle of crushed red pepper flakes.

Hands-On Time: 10 minutes
Cook Time: 10 minutes

Serves 4

1 (15-ounce) can chickpeas, drained and rinsed
2 cloves garlic, peeled
1 teaspoon ground cumin
¾ teaspoon salt
¼ teaspoon ground black pepper
2 tablespoons all-purpose flour
3 tablespoon olive oil

1 Preheat air fryer to 400°F.

2 Place chickpeas, garlic, cumin, salt, and pepper in a food processor and pulse ten times, or until chickpeas are coarsely blended, with some small chunks. Add flour to mixture and pulse three more times, until flour is incorporated.

3 Scoop out 2 tablespoons of mixture and shape into a patty about 2" in diameter. Repeat with remaining mixture. Brush each patty lightly with olive oil and place in air fryer basket in a single layer.

4 Cook 10 minutes, turning halfway through cooking. When done, falafel centers will feel firm and edges will be lightly browned and crispy. Let cool 5 minutes and serve warm.

PER SERVING

CALORIES: 195 | FAT: 11g | SODIUM: 572mg | CARBOHYDRATES: 18g | FIBER: 4g | SUGAR: 3g | PROTEIN: 5g

Balsamic Zucchini Boats

This recipe lets the natural flavors of zucchini shine. With a tomato topping and a sweet and tart balsamic glaze, this dish is perfect for those looking for a simple and fresh-tasting dish.

Hands-On Time: 10 minutes
Cook Time: 12 minutes

Serves 4

4 medium zucchini
1 cup grape tomatoes, quartered
4 tablespoons olive oil
1 teaspoon Italian seasoning
1 teaspoon salt
½ cup balsamic glaze
6 small fresh basil leaves, thinly sliced

THE DIFFERENCE BETWEEN BALSAMIC VINEGAR AND BALSAMIC GLAZE

Balsamic glaze is much thicker and sweeter than balsamic vinegar. It's a cooked-down version of balsamic vinegar, so its tangy flavor is more concentrated. Balsamic glaze also often contains some added sugar for sweetness.

1 Preheat air fryer to 350°F. Remove ends of zucchini and cut each in half lengthwise. Use a spoon to scoop out seeds, leaving a small area to be stuffed with tomatoes.

2 Place tomatoes inside each zucchini boat and drizzle with olive oil. Sprinkle with Italian seasoning and salt. Place boats in air fryer basket and cook 12 minutes. When done, zucchini will be fork-tender.

3 Garnish with balsamic glaze and basil to serve.

PER SERVING

CALORIES: 255 | FAT: 14g | SODIUM: 597mg | CARBOHYDRATES: 35g | FIBER: 2g | SUGAR: 33g | PROTEIN: 2g

Mushroom and Spinach Frittata

Frittatas are packed with protein and are a great meal option any time. This version is filled with fluffy eggs, umami-rich mushrooms, and tender vegetables. This recipe also works as a versatile, flavorful base to which you can add whichever leftover chopped vegetables and herbs strike your fancy.

Hands-On Time: 5 minutes
Cook Time: 20 minutes

Serves 4

6 large eggs
¼ cup whole milk
1 cup chopped cremini mushrooms (also called baby bellas)
1 cup firmly packed fresh spinach, chopped
½ cup chopped yellow onion
½ teaspoon salt
¼ teaspoon ground black pepper

1 Preheat air fryer to 350°F. Spray a 6" round baking pan with cooking spray and set aside.

2 In a large bowl, whisk together eggs and milk until well combined. Mix in mushrooms, spinach, onion, salt, and pepper.

3 Pour mixture into prepared pan and scrape all vegetables into pan. Cook 20 minutes, until eggs are fully cooked and firm in center. Serve warm.

PER SERVING

CALORIES: 130 | FAT: 7g | SODIUM: 411mg | CARBOHYDRATES: 4g | FIBER: 1g | SUGAR: 2g | PROTEIN: 11g

Avocado-Topped Sweet Potato Slices

This recipe is a fuss-free version of the sweet potato toast so many have come to love in the past several years. It features thick sweet potato slices coated with a smoky spice rub. The crisp slices perfectly complement the nutty qualities of avocado for a satisfying meal.

Hands-On Time: 5 minutes
Cook Time: 15 minutes

Serves 4

1 tablespoon olive oil
2 large sweet potatoes, peeled and sliced lengthwise into ¼"-thick ovals
1 teaspoon salt, divided
½ teaspoon chili powder
¼ teaspoon paprika
¼ teaspoon garlic powder
2 medium avocados, pitted, peeled, and mashed
¼ teaspoon crushed red pepper flakes

1 Preheat air fryer to 380°F.

2 Brush olive oil on both sides of each sweet potato slice. In a small bowl, mix ½ teaspoon salt, chili powder, paprika, and garlic powder until well combined. Sprinkle mixture evenly on both sides of each sweet potato slice.

3 Place slices in air fryer basket and cook 15 minutes, turning halfway through cooking time. When done, sweet potato slices will be browned and tender.

4 In a small bowl, mix remaining ½ teaspoon salt with mashed avocados and spread evenly on top of each sweet potato slice. Sprinkle with red pepper flakes and serve.

PER SERVING

CALORIES: 225 | FAT: 13g | SODIUM: 628mg | CARBOHYDRATES: 25g | FIBER: 8g | SUGAR: 6g | PROTEIN: 3g

Potato Tacos

Golden, crispy spiced potatoes are a budget-friendly taco filling for a delicious taco meal the whole family can enjoy. It's very easy to make a big batch to feed a group with this unique meat-free meal—and potatoes complement a range of flavors, so set out all kinds of toppings and let everyone choose their favorites.

Hands-On Time: 5 minutes
Cook Time: 12 minutes

Yields 12

4 cups frozen diced potatoes
2 tablespoons olive oil
½ teaspoon salt
½ teaspoon chili powder
¼ teaspoon paprika
¼ teaspoon garlic powder
¼ teaspoon ground black pepper
12 (4") flour tortillas, warmed
½ cup sour cream

CHIPOTLE SOUR CREAM

If you're a fan of smoky flavors, add 2 to 3 tablespoons of blended chipotles in adobo sauce to ½ cup of sour cream and a teaspoon of lime juice for an easy sauce with some kick.

1 Preheat air fryer to 400°F. Place potatoes in a large bowl and drizzle with olive oil. Sprinkle salt, chili powder, paprika, garlic powder, and pepper on top of potatoes and toss to coat.

2 Scrape potatoes into a 6" round baking pan and place in air fryer basket. Cook 12 minutes, stirring twice during cooking time. When done, potatoes will be fork-tender and browned.

3 Place a scoop of potatoes in center of each tortilla, then fold tortilla in half over filling. Top each with sour cream and serve.

PER SERVING (SERVING SIZE: 3 TACOS)

CALORIES: 513 | FAT: 18g | SODIUM: 1,004mg | CARBOHYDRATES: 76g | FIBER: 5g | SUGAR: 4g | PROTEIN: 11g

Spicy Cauliflower Wraps

Cauliflower has a mild taste, making it an excellent canvas for all your favorite flavors. Hot sauce gives these tender-crisp cauliflower bites a makeover, and they become a bold wrap filling that's worthy of being the center of attention. Fresh vegetables add crunch and brightness to this simple-to-make meal.

Hands-On Time: 5 minutes
Cook Time: 12 minutes

Serves 4

- 2 cups fresh cauliflower florets, chopped into bite-sized pieces
- 3 tablespoons olive oil
- 1 teaspoon salt
- ¼ teaspoon ground black pepper
- ½ cup hot sauce
- 1 cup shredded carrots
- 4 (8") flour tortillas, warmed
- 3 cups chopped romaine lettuce

1 Preheat air fryer to 400°F. Place cauliflower in a medium bowl. Drizzle with olive oil and sprinkle with salt and pepper, then toss to coat evenly.

2 Place cauliflower in air fryer basket and cook 12 minutes, shaking basket halfway through cooking time. When done, cauliflower will be tender and browned at edges.

3 While still warm, place cauliflower in a clean medium bowl and add hot sauce, then toss to evenly coat. Place ¼ cup shredded carrots in the center of each tortilla, and top each with ¼ of the spicy cauliflower and ¾ cup romaine. Fold in ends and wrap tortillas around vegetables, then cut diagonally in half to serve.

PER SERVING

CALORIES: 264 | **FAT:** 13g | **SODIUM:** 1,888mg | **CARBOHYDRATES:** 32g | **FIBER:** 4g | **SUGAR:** 5g | **PROTEIN:** 6g

Mushroom Veggie Burgers

You might be surprised to know that homemade veggie burgers are very simple to make. With the help of a food processor, you can craft fresh ingredients into a savory burger that's full of flavor and tastes much more fresh than its frozen equivalent. Add your favorite burger toppings, such as crunchy red onion rings, leafy lettuce, or a juicy slice of tomato, for a delicious and satisfying meal.

Hands-On Time: 10 minutes
Cook Time: 15 minutes

Serves 4

- 8 ounces cremini mushrooms (also called baby bellas), stems removed
- 1 (15-ounce) can chickpeas, drained and rinsed
- ½ cup Italian-style bread crumbs
- ¼ cup chopped white onion
- 2 cloves garlic, peeled
- 1 tablespoon soy sauce
- ½ teaspoon smoked paprika
- ½ teaspoon salt
- 4 white burger buns

1 Preheat air fryer to 400°F. Place all ingredients except buns in a food processor and pulse ten times, until mixture breaks down into small pieces and begins to stick together.

2 Divide mixture into 4 equal portions. Shape each portion into a patty 5" in diameter. Place patties in air fryer basket and cook 15 minutes, turning halfway through cooking. When done, patties will be firm and hold together easily.

3 Place on buns and serve warm.

PER SERVING

CALORIES: 282 | **FAT:** 3g | **SODIUM:** 1,058mg | **CARBOHYDRATES:** 50g | **FIBER:** 6g | **SUGAR:** 8g | **PROTEIN:** 13g

Shredded Barbecue Mushrooms

These mushrooms mimic the texture of pulled pork, making them the perfect meat-free addition to your barbecue buffet. You can enjoy these flavorful, tender mushroom shreds alone or put them on a toasted burger bun.

Hands-On Time: 5 minutes
Cook Time: 10 minutes

Serves 4

4 king oyster mushrooms (also called king trumpet mushrooms)
1 tablespoon olive oil
1 teaspoon chili powder
½ teaspoon paprika
½ teaspoon garlic powder
½ teaspoon salt
¼ teaspoon ground black pepper
½ cup barbecue sauce

MUSHROOM SWAP

King oyster mushrooms, also called king trumpet mushrooms, shred easily with a fork and are perfect for this recipe, but if you have trouble finding them, you can also use large portobello mushrooms as an alternative.

1 Preheat air fryer to 400°F. Brush each mushroom all over with olive oil and sprinkle evenly with chili powder, paprika, garlic powder, salt, and pepper.

2 Place mushrooms in air fryer basket and cook 8 minutes.

3 Use tongs or a spatula to transfer mushrooms to a cutting board. Use two forks to gently pull apart mushrooms, creating strands.

4 Place mushroom strands in a 6" round baking pan and add barbecue sauce, then toss to coat. Place pan in air fryer basket and cook 2 minutes. When done, mushrooms will be tender and browned. Serve warm.

PER SERVING

CALORIES: 143 | FAT: 4g | SODIUM: 703mg | CARBOHYDRATES: 24g | FIBER: 4g | SUGAR: 14g | PROTEIN: 5g

9

Desserts

If you need something sweet in order to feel truly satisfied after your meal, this chapter will be your go-to guide for quick and easy desserts. Not only are these recipes simple to make, but they come together in no time so that you can appease your sweet tooth almost as quickly as the craving comes. From dressed-up delights like Fried Oreos to unique treats like Cheesecake Wontons, this chapter has goodies to fit every taste and appetite!

Spiced Apple Turnovers

This one's for the pie lovers who can't get enough crust. In this recipe, simple apple pie filling is surrounded by a flaky, golden puff pastry crust drizzled in sweet icing. The filling-to-crust ratio ensures both apple flavor and buttery crunch are always in the mix.

Hands-On Time: 10 minutes
Cook Time: 15 minutes

Serves 4

1 cup canned apple pie filling
½ teaspoon apple pie spice
1 (13.2-ounce) package puff pastry, thawed
1 large egg, whisked
½ cup confectioners' sugar
2 tablespoons whole milk

WHAT'S IN APPLE PIE SPICE?

Similar to pumpkin pie spice, apple pie spice is a convenient aromatic blend of spices. Apple pie spice mixes vary, but they often combine cinnamon, ginger, nutmeg, and/or allspice. For added depth, seek out a mix that has cardamom too.

1 Preheat air fryer to 350°F. Place apple pie filling in a medium bowl, sprinkle with apple pie spice, mix, then set aside.

2 On a clean work surface, cut puff pastry into 4 even squares. Turnovers will be folded diagonally, so place apple pie mixture slightly off-center on each pastry piece, leaving a ½" border at the edges. Brush edges with egg, then fold each square into a triangle to enclose filling. Press edges closed and crimp with a fork. Lightly brush top of each pastry with egg.

3 Place turnovers in air fryer and cook 15 minutes, turning when 5 minutes of cooking time remain. When done, pastry will be golden brown and flaky. Allow to cool 5 minutes.

4 In a small bowl, whisk together sugar and milk. Drizzle onto turnovers. Serve warm.

PER SERVING

CALORIES: 561 | FAT: 24g | SODIUM: 409mg | CARBOHYDRATES: 81g | FIBER: 2g | SUGAR: 34g | PROTEIN: 7g

Caramelized Pineapple

This versatile dessert enhances the natural flavor of pineapple with a bit of added warmth. You can enjoy it served over vanilla ice cream, as a cake topping, or even with a spoon by itself!

Hands-On Time: 5 minutes
Cook Time: 5 minutes

Serves 4

2 (20-ounce) cans pineapple slices, drained
2 tablespoons salted butter, melted
¼ cup light brown sugar, packed
2 teaspoons ground cinnamon

1 Preheat air fryer to 400°F. Cut each pineapple slice into 4 even pieces and place in a large bowl.

2 Pour butter over pineapple pieces and sprinkle with brown sugar and cinnamon. Toss to coat. Place pineapple pieces in air fryer basket and cook 5 minutes, turning halfway through cooking. When done, pineapple pieces will be gooey and browned. Serve warm.

PER SERVING

CALORIES: 277 | **FAT:** 6g | **SODIUM:** 52mg | **CARBOHYDRATES:** 59g | **FIBER:** 4g | **SUGAR:** 54g | **PROTEIN:** 2g

Bread Pudding

Don't throw out your day-old bread! This custard-based dessert is the perfect way to use it—a rich and creamy sweet treat that bakes up in no time. Enjoy this dish warm or chilled straight from the refrigerator for a quick and simple treat.

Hands-On Time: 10 minutes
Cook Time: 20 minutes

Serves 4

2 large eggs
1½ cups whole milk
⅓ cup granulated sugar
1 teaspoon ground cinnamon
2 teaspoons vanilla extract
4 cups ½" brioche cubes
2 tablespoons confectioners' sugar

1 Preheat air fryer to 350°F. In a large bowl, whisk together eggs, milk, sugar, cinnamon, and vanilla until well combined. Place brioche in mixture and let soak 5 minutes.

2 Lightly spray a 6" round baking pan with cooking spray and scrape mixture into pan. Cook 20 minutes, until top is browned and center is firm. Dust with confectioners' sugar and serve warm or chilled.

PER SERVING

CALORIES: 323 | **FAT:** 7g | **SODIUM:** 324mg | **CARBOHYDRATES:** 54g | **FIBER:** 0g | **SUGAR:** 29g | **PROTEIN:** 10g

Fried Oreos

Bring the fun and tasty goodness of the county fair right to your own kitchen with these chocolatey delights. This recipe simplifies the fried and battered treat into a sweet, crispy homemade version that's ready in just minutes!

Hands-On Time: 5 minutes
Cook Time: 8 minutes

Serves 8

1 (8-ounce) tube refrigerated crescent roll dough
8 Oreo cookies
¼ cup confectioners' sugar

1 Preheat air fryer to 350°F. Roll dough out on a work surface, and press all seams together. Cut dough into 8 even pieces.

2 Place an Oreo at center of each piece of dough. Fold dough around Oreo and gather edges, pressing dough together to fully enclose each cookie.

3 Spray each cookie lightly with cooking spray and place in air fryer basket. Cook 8 minutes, turning halfway through cooking time. When done, Oreos will be golden brown. Allow 5 minutes to cool, then dust with confectioners' sugar. Serve warm.

PER SERVING

CALORIES: 168 | FAT: 7g | SODIUM: 259mg | CARBOHYDRATES: 24g | FIBER: 0g | SUGAR: 11g | PROTEIN: 3g

White Chocolate and Strawberry Cake Mix Cookies

You can make some of the easiest, moistest, and most delicious cookies by starting with a simple box of cake mix. The dense, flavorful result is a cake-cookie hybrid in a bite-sized form that you'll be reaching for over and over again.

Hands-On Time: 5 minutes
Cook Time: 10 minutes

Yields 12

1 (18.5-ounce) box strawberry cake mix
2 large eggs
½ cup unsalted butter, melted
½ cup white chocolate chips

SWITCH UP THE FLAVORS

This recipe is made with strawberry cake mix, but feel free to swap it for vanilla or even chocolate cake. This recipe makes an excellent base for a wide range of flavors, so get creative!

1 Preheat air fryer to 350°F. Cut two pieces of parchment paper to fit air fryer and set aside.

2 In a large bowl, whisk together cake mix, eggs, and butter until well combined. Fold in chocolate chips. Scoop up 2 tablespoons of dough and roll into a ball, then flatten into a disc ½" thick. Repeat with remaining dough.

3 Place cookies on parchment, leaving 2" of space between each. Working in batches as needed, place parchment in air fryer basket. Cook 10 minutes, until golden at edges, then transfer to a wire rack to cool 5 minutes. Serve warm.

PER SERVING (SERVING SIZE: 1 COOKIE)

CALORIES: 280 | FAT: 11g | SODIUM: 334mg | CARBOHYDRATES: 41g | FIBER: 0g | SUGAR: 24g | PROTEIN: 4g

Cheesecake Wontons

A traditional cheesecake recipe takes several hours from when you remove the cream cheese from the refrigerator to the moment the cheesecake is ready to eat. This recipe delivers a handheld version with all of the same sweet and creamy flavors and luscious textures in less than 20 minutes!

Hands-On Time: 10 minutes
Cook Time: 8 minutes

Serves 4

- 4 ounces cream cheese, softened
- 2 tablespoons sour cream
- ¼ cup granulated sugar
- 1 teaspoon vanilla extract
- 12 (3" × 3") wonton wrappers
- ¼ cup water

ADD FRUIT!

Chop up berries and mix into the cheesecake for a fruity twist! Alternatively, you can top the finished wontons with premade fruit sauce and whipped cream for an ultra-decadent plate.

1 Preheat air fryer to 375°F. In a medium bowl, beat cream cheese, sour cream, sugar, and vanilla until light and fluffy, about 3 minutes.

2 Place 2 teaspoons of cheesecake mixture in center of each wonton wrapper. Brush edges with water. Fold two opposing corners of the wonton wrapper to meet in center, covering cream cheese, and pinch to close. Repeat with the remaining two corners.

3 Lightly spray wontons with cooking spray and place in air fryer basket. Cook 8 minutes, until golden brown and crispy. Serve warm.

PER SERVING

CALORIES: 229 | **FAT:** 10g | **SODIUM:** 243mg | **CARBOHYDRATES:** 28g | **FIBER:** 0g | **SUGAR:** 14g | **PROTEIN:** 4g

Cherry Cobbler

This comfort food is easier than ever to whip up with a can of pie filling and a handful of pantry staples. You can bake this golden brown dessert in less than 30 minutes with minimal effort. Satisfying bursts of cherries and sweet sauce make this dessert extra-sweet and contrast nicely with the buttery cobbler crust.

Hands-On Time: 5 minutes
Cook Time: 20 minutes

Serves 6

2 (21-ounce) cans cherry pie filling
½ cup all-purpose flour
⅓ cup granulated sugar
1 teaspoon baking powder
¼ teaspoon salt
1 teaspoon vanilla extract
⅓ cup whole milk
4 tablespoons salted butter, melted
1 large egg

1 Preheat air fryer to 350°F. Lightly spray a 6" round baking pan with cooking spray and scrape cherry pie filling into pan.

2 In a medium bowl, whisk together flour, sugar, baking powder, and salt until well combined. Mix in vanilla, milk, butter, and egg until a biscuit-type dough forms. Drop spoonfuls of topping on cherries to cover as well as possible.

3 Place pan in air fryer basket and cook 20 minutes. When done, topping will be browned and cherry filling will be bubbling at edges. Serve warm.

PER SERVING

CALORIES: 361 | FAT: 8g | SODIUM: 292mg | CARBOHYDRATES: 68g | FIBER: 1g | SUGAR: 12g | PROTEIN: 2g

Caramel Apple Crumble

This easy-to-put-together dessert includes tart, crisp apples seasoned to perfection and finished with buttery, crunchy streusel topping. Baking in only 15 minutes, it's one of the simplest ways your apple harvest can become a sweet treat the whole family will love.

Hands-On Time: 10 minutes
Cook Time: 15 minutes

Serves 4

3 Granny Smith apples, cored and diced
¼ cup light brown sugar, packed
½ cup all-purpose flour
½ cup rolled oats
¼ cup unsalted butter, cut into small cubes
¼ cup caramel sauce

1 Preheat air fryer to 350°F. Spray four 4" ramekins with cooking spray and set aside.

2 In a large bowl, mix apples and brown sugar until combined. Scoop mixture evenly into ramekins.

3 In a medium bowl, whisk together flour and oats. Use a fork to work butter into flour mixture until small and medium crumbs form. Sprinkle ramekins with crumb topping.

4 Place ramekins in air fryer and bake 15 minutes, until topping is golden brown and apples are tender. Drizzle with caramel sauce, 1 tablespoon per ramekin, and serve warm.

PER SERVING

CALORIES: 372 | **FAT:** 12g | **SODIUM:** 78mg | **CARBOHYDRATES:** 63g | **FIBER:** 5g | **SUGAR:** 26g | **PROTEIN:** 4g

Baked Peaches

This recipe builds on the natural sweetness of peaches to transform the summery fruit into an indulgent treat. The peaches' warm, spiced flavors pair with cold, creamy ice cream to make this dessert a crowd-pleasing delight.

Hands-On Time: 5 minutes
Cook Time: 10 minutes

Serves 4

- 4 medium peaches, halved, pits removed
- 2 tablespoons unsalted butter, melted
- ¼ cup light brown sugar, packed
- 2 teaspoons ground cinnamon
- 2 cups vanilla ice cream
- 4 sprigs fresh mint

1 Preheat air fryer to 320°F. Brush each peach half with butter and sprinkle with brown sugar and cinnamon.

2 Place peaches in air fryer basket, cut sides up, and cook 10 minutes, until soft and caramelized. To serve, divide peaches into small bowls alongside vanilla ice cream. Garnish each ice cream scoop with 1 mint sprig. Serve warm.

PER SERVING

CALORIES: 301 | **FAT:** 12g | **SODIUM:** 57mg | **CARBOHYDRATES:** 44g | **FIBER:** 3g | **SUGAR:** 40g | **PROTEIN:** 4g

Pumpkin Coffee Cake

It's never been easier to capture all of the warm and comforting spiced flavors of autumn. This simple pumpkin cake is your shortcut to a moist and flavorful dessert finished with the classic crumb topping you know and love. You can even get away with enjoying a slice for breakfast!

Hands-On Time: 5 minutes
Cook Time: 20 minutes

Yields 2 (6") cakes, serves 12

1 (15.2-ounce) box spice cake mix
2 large eggs
1 (15-ounce) can pumpkin purée
¾ cup all-purpose flour
1 tablespoon ground cinnamon
¼ cup salted butter, melted

FREEZER-FRIENDLY

This coffee cake uses premade cake mix and yields two 6" cakes in order to use all the batter. You can choose to enjoy both cakes or freeze one for later. To freeze, allow the cake to cool completely. Then wrap it tightly in plastic wrap, then in aluminum foil, and place in a 1-gallon freezer-safe sealable bag. To thaw, simply place the cake in the refrigerator overnight.

1 Preheat air fryer to 320°F. Line two 6" round baking pans with parchment paper and spray with cooking spray, then set aside.

2 In a large bowl, whisk together cake mix, eggs, and pumpkin until a smooth batter forms. Divide batter evenly between prepared pans.

3 In a medium bowl, whisk together flour, cinnamon, and butter until medium crumbs form. Sprinkle crumbs on top of each cake. Working in batches, place cake in air fryer basket and cook 20 minutes, until a toothpick inserted in center comes out clean. Serve warm.

PER SERVING

CALORIES: 237 | **FAT:** 7g | **SODIUM:** 264mg | **CARBOHYDRATES:** 28g | **FIBER:** 2g | **SUGAR:** 17g | **PROTEIN:** 3g

Mini Peach Upside-Down Cupcakes

Moist, summery, and easy to make, these cupcakes are a great weeknight dessert. Crammed with cinnamon flavor and juicy peaches, they are a delicious simplified spin on pineapple upside-down cake. Top with your choice of a mound of whipped cream, a scoop of creamy vanilla ice cream, or simply a drizzle of honey for a sweet treat that doesn't take a lot of effort.

Hands-On Time: 5 minutes
Cook Time: 12 minutes

Serves 12

- 1 (15.2-ounce) box yellow cake mix
- 1 large egg
- ½ cup vegetable oil
- ⅓ cup light brown sugar, packed
- 1 teaspoon ground cinnamon
- 2 cups drained canned peach chunks

1 Preheat air fryer to 320°F. Spray 12 silicone cupcake liners with cooking spray and set aside.

2 In a large bowl, whisk together cake mix, egg, and vegetable oil until well combined. In a small bowl, mix brown sugar, cinnamon, and peach chunks until well combined.

3 Place 1 tablespoon of peach mixture in bottom of each cupcake liner and spread in an even layer. Spoon ¼ cup of batter over each cup of peaches. Place cupcakes in air fryer basket, working in batches as needed. Cook 12 minutes, until each cake is lightly browned and a toothpick inserted in center comes out clean. Let cool 10 minutes.

4 Invert cupcakes onto small dessert plates and serve warm. Store leftover cupcakes in the refrigerator in an airtight container for up to 3 days.

PER SERVING

CALORIES: 293 | **FAT:** 13g | **SODIUM:** 245mg | **CARBOHYDRATES:** 41g | **FIBER:** 1g | **SUGAR:** 11g | **PROTEIN:** 2g

Pumpkin Donut Holes

These donut holes have got fall flavor covered. The batter relies on pure pumpkin purée rather than eggs as a binder, and this substitution not only holds the donuts together well but also gives them concentrated pumpkin flavor. They come together quickly and only require a few ingredients. These soft and fluffy bites are sure to be a hit!

Hands-On Time: 5 minutes
Cook Time: 7 minutes

Serves 4

¾ cup pure pumpkin purée
½ cup whole milk
2 cups all-purpose baking mix (such as Bisquick)
2 teaspoons pumpkin pie spice, divided
½ cup granulated sugar, divided
2 tablespoons salted butter, melted

1 Preheat air fryer to 380°F. Cut a piece of parchment paper to fit air fryer basket and set aside. In a large bowl, mix pumpkin purée, milk, baking mix, 1 teaspoon pumpkin pie spice, and ¼ cup sugar until a thick batter forms.

2 Scoop 1-tablespoon portions of batter onto parchment paper and place in air fryer basket. Cook 7 minutes, turning when 2 minutes of cooking time remain. When done, donut holes will be browned and a toothpick inserted in center will come out clean.

3 Place remaining 1 teaspoon pumpkin pie spice and remaining ¼ cup sugar in a small bowl and mix. Brush butter over each donut hole and roll in sugar mixture to coat. Serve.

PER SERVING

CALORIES: 427 | FAT: 13g | SODIUM: 675mg | CARBOHYDRATES: 70g | FIBER: 3g | SUGAR: 30g | PROTEIN: 6g

Blueberry Pie Bites

If you're craving something sweet but a whole pie is too much of a time commitment, these quick pie bites can be a satisfying dessert solution. Wild blueberries (often found in the freezer section) are smaller than cultivated ones, so they fit perfectly in these mini bites. If you keep the berries on hand, this can be a great spur-of-the-moment recipe. Feel free to use halved regular blueberries if that's what you have.

Hands-On Time: 10 minutes
Cook Time: 12 minutes

Yields 8

1 tablespoon cornstarch
¼ cup granulated sugar
2 teaspoons lemon juice
1 cup wild blueberries, fresh or thawed
1 (16-ounce) tube refrigerated biscuit dough
¼ cup confectioners' sugar

1 Preheat air fryer to 350°F. In a medium bowl, mix cornstarch, sugar, lemon juice, and blueberries, then set aside.

2 On a clean work surface, separate each biscuit into 2 even pieces. Gently press or roll each piece out to a 4" circle. Place 1 tablespoon blueberry filling in center of each circle. Gently stretch and pinch dough around filling until sealed, and shape into a ball.

3 Place bites in air fryer basket, seam sides down. Cook 12 minutes, turning when 3 minutes of cooking time remain. When done, bites will be browned and dough will be firm. Let cool 5 minutes, then dust with confectioners' sugar to serve.

PER SERVING (SERVING SIZE: 1 BITE)

CALORIES: 224 | FAT: 6g | SODIUM: 554mg | CARBOHYDRATES: 39g | FIBER: 1g | SUGAR: 15g | PROTEIN: 4g

Three-Ingredient Peanut Butter Cookies

With only three ingredients, you can make a batch of soft, chewy cookies in no time. Creamy peanut butter works best, but feel free to use chunky for a little more texture. You'll love the crunchy edges and soft centers that make these cookies so craveable.

Hands-On Time: 5 minutes
Cook Time: 8 minutes

Yields 8

1 cup creamy peanut butter
¾ cup confectioners' sugar
1 large egg, room
    temperature

CUSTOMIZE IT!
Feel free to add a dusting of sugar or some chocolate chips to the cookie dough. A small handful of semisweet chocolate chips or a dash of ground cinnamon can add a whole new depth of flavor.

1 Preheat air fryer to 350°F and cut a piece of parchment to fit air fryer basket.

2 In a large bowl, mix peanut butter, sugar, and egg until smooth and well combined. Use a 1" cookie scoop to form 8 cookie balls. Use the tines of a fork to gently press a criss-cross pattern into the top of each cookie.

3 Working in batches as needed, place cookies on parchment and place in air fryer basket. Cook 8 minutes, until cookies are browned at edges. Allow cookies to cool 5 minutes, then serve.

PER SERVING (SERVING SIZE: 1 COOKIE)

CALORIES: 238 | FAT: 16g | SODIUM: 14mg | CARBOHYDRATES: 17g | FIBER: 2g | SUGAR: 13g | PROTEIN: 8g

Banana Bites with Caramel Drizzle

When the bananas on your countertop have turned soft and are beginning to spot, it's time to bake up these delicious bites. They bring the flavors of banana pancakes and banana fritters together for a tasty dessert. Dusted with confectioners' sugar to accent the bananas' natural sweetness, these are perfect for all ages and ready in less than 20 minutes.

Hands-On Time: 10 minutes
Cook Time: 8 minutes

Serves 4

- 1½ cups all-purpose baking mix (such as Bisquick)
- ½ cup whole milk
- 1 large egg
- 3 medium bananas, peeled and cut into 1½"-thick chunks
- ¼ cup caramel sauce, warmed

1 Preheat air fryer to 400°F. Cut a piece of parchment paper to fit air fryer basket. In a large bowl, whisk together baking mix, milk, and egg.

2 Use a fork to pick up a chunk of banana, dip in batter to coat, and place on parchment. Repeat for all banana chunks. Carefully transfer bananas on parchment to air fryer basket and cook 8 minutes, turning halfway through cooking. When done, bananas will be lightly browned all over and feel firm to the touch.

3 Let cool 5 minutes, drizzle with caramel sauce, and serve warm.

PER SERVING

CALORIES: 346 | **FAT:** 7g | **SODIUM:** 564mg | **CARBOHYDRATES:** 65g | **FIBER:** 4g | **SUGAR:** 14g | **PROTEIN:** 7g

Chocolate Cupcakes

Whether you make them to celebrate a special day or simply to enjoy a decadent treat, these cupcakes are always a hit. They're moist, chocolate-forward, and air fried to perfection. This recipe uses a small amount of espresso powder to enhance the chocolate flavor, but feel free to leave it out. Top these cupcakes with your favorite store-bought frosting.

Hands-On Time: 5 minutes
Cook Time: 12 minutes

Yields 12

1 cup all-purpose flour
⅓ cup granulated sugar
¼ cup cocoa powder
½ teaspoon espresso powder
1 large egg, room
   temperature
½ cup vegetable oil
1 teaspoon vanilla extract
½ cup whole milk

1 Preheat air fryer to 320°F. Spray 12 silicone or aluminum cupcake liners with nonstick cooking spray.

2 In a large bowl, whisk together flour, sugar, cocoa powder, and espresso powder until combined. Whisk in egg, vegetable oil, vanilla, and milk until a mostly smooth batter forms.

3 Fill cupcake liners about halfway and place in air fryer basket, working in batches as needed. Cook 12 minutes, until cakes are firm at edges and a toothpick inserted in a center comes out mostly clean. Serve warm.

PER SERVING (SERVING SIZE: 1 CUPCAKE)

CALORIES: 159 | FAT: 10g | SODIUM: 10mg | CARBOHYDRATES: 15g | FIBER: 1g | SUGAR: 6g | PROTEIN: 2g

Flourless Oatmeal Chocolate Chip Cookie Bars

Oatmeal isn't just for breakfast. These simple cookie bars are soft, chewy, and oozing with gooey chocolate. Cinnamon adds depth to this sweet treat and gives the bars a warming flavor that you'll find yourself coming back to again and again.

Hands-On Time: 5 minutes
Cook Time: 22 minutes

Yields 8

- ½ cup light brown sugar, packed
- ½ cup light corn syrup
- 1 teaspoon vanilla extract
- ½ teaspoon salt
- 1 teaspoon ground cinnamon
- 1 cup quick-cooking oats
- 2 large eggs
- ¾ cup semisweet chocolate chips

1 Preheat air fryer to 320°F. Spray a 6" round baking pan with nonstick cooking spray and set aside.

2 In a large bowl, mix brown sugar, corn syrup, vanilla, salt, and cinnamon until well combined. Mix in oats and eggs until fully combined, then fold in chocolate chips.

3 Scrape mixture into prepared baking pan. Place pan in air fryer basket. Bake 22 minutes, or until a toothpick inserted in center comes out clean. Let cool 5 minutes before serving.

PER SERVING (SERVING SIZE: 1 BAR)

CALORIES: 252 | FAT: 7g | SODIUM: 182mg | CARBOHYDRATES: 48g | FIBER: 2g | SUGAR: 39g | PROTEIN: 4g

Individual Vanilla Cakes

This simple vanilla cake recipe mixes up in minutes and only requires one bowl. It's fluffy and tender, with a striking vanilla taste. If you're not in the mood for vanilla, you can easily swap out the vanilla extract for cake batter extract, almond extract, or even coconut extract. Here, the cakes are topped with whipped cream for a light and easy option, but you could choose to grab a tub of frosting at the store for a creamier topping.

Hands-On Time: 5 minutes
Cook Time: 15 minutes

Serves 4

- ½ cup self-rising flour
- ¼ cup granulated sugar
- ¼ cup whole milk
- 2 tablespoons unsalted butter, melted
- 1 teaspoon vanilla extract
- 1 large egg, room temperature
- 1 cup whipped cream

1 Preheat air fryer to 320°F. Spray four 4" ramekins with nonstick cooking spray and set aside.

2 Mix all ingredients except whipped cream in a large bowl until smooth. Separate batter evenly among ramekins.

3 Place ramekins in air fryer basket and cook 15 minutes, until tops are browned and a toothpick inserted in a cake's center comes out mostly clean. Allow 10 minutes to cool, then top with whipped cream to serve.

PER SERVING

CALORIES: 222 | FAT: 10g | SODIUM: 212mg | CARBOHYDRATES: 27g | FIBER: 0g | SUGAR: 15g | PROTEIN: 4g

Mini Raspberry Turnovers

Layers of crispy, golden puff pastry give this dessert an amazing crunch. Raspberry preserves add a sweet and tart fruity flavor, but feel free to swap out raspberry for peach or apricot.

Hands-On Time: 10 minutes
Cook Time: 10 minutes

Yields 6

1 (13.2-ounce) package puff pastry, thawed
¾ cup raspberry preserves
1 large egg, whisked

SIMPLE GLAZE

If you like a sweet glaze on your turnovers, whisk together 1 cup confectioners' sugar and 3 tablespoons milk until smooth. Drizzle over cooled turnovers and serve.

1 Preheat air fryer to 350°F. Cut two pieces of parchment paper to fit air fryer basket.

2 Unroll puff pastry and place on a clean work surface. Cut into 6 even rectangles. Place 2 tablespoons preserves in center of each rectangle.

3 Fold over each rectangle and press edges together firmly to seal. Use tip of a knife to cut three slits into top of each turnover.

4 Brush each turnover with egg and place in air fryer basket. Cook 10 minutes, carefully turning when 2 minutes remain. Turnovers will be golden brown when done. Let cool 5 minutes before serving.

PER SERVING (SERVING SIZE: 1 TURNOVER)

CALORIES: 351 | **FAT:** 16g | **SODIUM:** 237mg | **CARBOHYDRATES:** 47g | **FIBER:** 0g | **SUGAR:** 20g | **PROTEIN:** 4g

Nutella-Stuffed Crescent Rolls

This dish couldn't be easier to make, and it's ready in less than 15 minutes. The soft, buttery crescent rolls make the perfect canvas for the extra-sweet chocolate hazelnut spread, creating a balanced dessert that the whole family will enjoy.

Hands-On Time: 5 minutes
Cook Time: 8 minutes

Yields 8

1 (8-ounce) tube refrigerated crescent roll dough
½ cup Nutella chocolate hazelnut spread

1 Preheat air fryer to 320°F.

2 On a clean work surface, unroll dough and separate into triangles. Place 1 tablespoon Nutella near the widest edge of each triangle. Roll each piece of dough toward pointed end to form roll.

3 Place rolls in air fryer basket and bake 8 minutes, until golden brown. Let cool 5 minutes and serve.

PER SERVING (SERVING SIZE: 2 ROLLS)

CALORIES: 402 | FAT: 21g | SODIUM: 440mg | CARBOHYDRATES: 46g | FIBER: 1g | SUGAR: 27g | PROTEIN: 7g

Strawberry Galette

If you love pie but not the work that goes into baking it, this fruity galette is for you. In just 10 minutes you can prep this delicious summery dessert. You'll love how golden and delicious the crust turns in the air fryer, but the filling is the real star of this dish. Fresh strawberries give the galette just the right amount of sweetness. Enjoy a slice alone or with a scoop of vanilla ice cream on the side.

Hands-On Time: 10 minutes
Cook Time: 20 minutes

Serves 6

- 2 cups fresh strawberries, hulled and cut into ¼"-thick slices
- ¼ cup granulated sugar
- 2 tablespoons cornstarch
- 1 teaspoon vanilla extract
- 1 (9") pie dough round
- 1 large egg, whisked

RUSTIC PRESENTATION

This dish is meant to have a rustic look, so don't worry too much about the pleats. Just be sure to leave 3"–4" of strawberries exposed in the center, and embrace the free-form look for this tasty fruit dish.

1 Preheat air fryer to 350°F. Cut a piece of parchment to fit air fryer basket. In a medium bowl, combine strawberries, sugar, cornstarch, and vanilla.

2 Unroll pie dough onto precut parchment paper. Scrape strawberry mixture into center of pie crust and spread on crust, leaving a 2" border around edges. Gently fold up border edges of crust, creating pleats as you go and keeping strawberries in center uncovered, as with a traditional galette.

3 Use a pastry brush to coat crust with egg wash. Transfer galette on parchment to air fryer basket and bake 20 minutes, until dark golden brown and bubbling. Let cool 5 minutes before slicing. Serve warm.

PER SERVING

CALORIES: 204 | FAT: 9g | SODIUM: 185mg | CARBOHYDRATES: 31g | FIBER: 1g | SUGAR: 11g | PROTEIN: 2g

Chocolate Chip Cookie Cake

When cookies themselves don't feel grand enough, a cookie cake can be the perfect solution for an elevated treat. Brown sugar gives this cookie cake a caramelized, deep flavor that makes this soft and gooey cake a pure delight. For a quick decoration, feel free to pick up a tube of icing and pipe a design around the edges, or add some sprinkles for a birthday-worthy treat.

Hands-On Time: 5 minutes
Cook Time: 15 minutes

Serves 4

½ cup unsalted butter, melted
½ cup light brown sugar, packed
1 cup all-purpose flour
¼ teaspoon salt
1 large egg, room temperature
1 teaspoon baking powder
1 teaspoon vanilla extract
½ cup semisweet chocolate chips

1 Preheat air fryer to 350°F. Spray a 6" round baking pan with nonstick cooking spray and set aside.

2 In a large bowl, stir butter, brown sugar, flour, salt, egg, baking powder, and vanilla until well combined. Gently fold in chocolate chips.

3 Scoop batter into pan and press down gently to spread evenly. Cook 15 minutes, until top and center are golden brown and a toothpick inserted in center comes out mostly clean. Serve warm.

PER SERVING

CALORIES: 552 | FAT: 29g | SODIUM: 298mg | CARBOHYDRATES: 66g | FIBER: 2g | SUGAR: 39g | PROTEIN: 6g

US/Metric Conversion Chart

VOLUME CONVERSIONS

US Volume Measure	Metric Equivalent
⅛ teaspoon	0.5 milliliter
¼ teaspoon	1 milliliter
½ teaspoon	2 milliliters
1 teaspoon	5 milliliters
½ tablespoon	7 milliliters
1 tablespoon (3 teaspoons)	15 milliliters
2 tablespoons (1 fluid ounce)	30 milliliters
¼ cup (4 tablespoons)	60 milliliters
⅓ cup	90 milliliters
½ cup (4 fluid ounces)	125 milliliters
⅔ cup	160 milliliters
¾ cup (6 fluid ounces)	180 milliliters
1 cup (16 tablespoons)	250 milliliters
1 pint (2 cups)	500 milliliters
1 quart (4 cups)	1 liter (about)

WEIGHT CONVERSIONS

US Weight Measure	Metric Equivalent
½ ounce	15 grams
1 ounce	30 grams
2 ounces	60 grams
3 ounces	85 grams
¼ pound (4 ounces)	115 grams
½ pound (8 ounces)	225 grams
¾ pound (12 ounces)	340 grams
1 pound (16 ounces)	454 grams

OVEN TEMPERATURE CONVERSIONS

Degrees Fahrenheit	Degrees Celsius
200 degrees F	95 degrees C
250 degrees F	120 degrees C
275 degrees F	135 degrees C
300 degrees F	150 degrees C
325 degrees F	160 degrees C
350 degrees F	180 degrees C
375 degrees F	190 degrees C
400 degrees F	205 degrees C
425 degrees F	220 degrees C
450 degrees F	230 degrees C

BAKING PAN SIZES

American	Metric
8 x 1½ inch round baking pan	20 x 4 cm cake tin
9 x 1½ inch round baking pan	23 x 3.5 cm cake tin
11 x 7 x 1½ inch baking pan	28 x 18 x 4 cm baking tin
13 x 9 x 2 inch baking pan	30 x 20 x 5 cm baking tin
2 quart rectangular baking dish	30 x 20 x 3 cm baking tin
15 x 10 x 2 inch baking pan	30 x 25 x 2 cm baking tin (Swiss roll tin)
9 inch pie plate	22 x 4 or 23 x 4 cm pie plate
7 or 8 inch springform pan	18 or 20 cm springform or loose bottom cake tin
9 x 5 x 3 inch loaf pan	23 x 13 x 7 cm or 2 lb narrow loaf or pâté tin
1½ quart casserole	1.5 liter casserole
2 quart casserole	2 liter casserole

Index